Lecture Notes in Computer Science 15730

Founding Editors

Gerhard Goos
Juris Hartmanis

Series Editors

Elisa Bertino, *Purdue University, West Lafayette, IN, USA*
Wen Gao, *Peking University, Beijing, China*
Bernhard Steffen, *TU Dortmund University, Dortmund, Germany*
Moti Yung, *Columbia University, New York, NY, USA*

The series Lecture Notes in Computer Science (LNCS), including its subseries Lecture Notes in Artificial Intelligence (LNAI) and Lecture Notes in Bioinformatics (LNBI), has established itself as a medium for the publication of new developments in computer science and information technology research, teaching, and education.

LNCS enjoys close cooperation with the computer science R & D community, the series counts many renowned academics among its volume editors and paper authors, and collaborates with prestigious societies. Its mission is to serve this international community by providing an invaluable service, mainly focused on the publication of conference and workshop proceedings and postproceedings. LNCS commenced publication in 1973.

Daniel Balouek · Ibéria Medeiros
Editors

Distributed Applications and Interoperable Systems

25th IFIP WG 6.1 International Conference, DAIS 2025
Held as Part of the 20th International Federated Conference
on Distributed Computing Techniques, DisCoTec 2025
Lille, France, June 16–20, 2025
Proceedings

Editors
Daniel Balouek
Inria
Rennes, France

Ibéria Medeiros
University of Lisbon
Lisbon, Portugal

ISSN 0302-9743   ISSN 1611-3349 (electronic)
Lecture Notes in Computer Science
ISBN 978-3-031-95727-7   ISBN 978-3-031-95728-4 (eBook)
https://doi.org/10.1007/978-3-031-95728-4

© IFIP International Federation for Information Processing 2025

This work is subject to copyright. All rights are solely and exclusively licensed by the Publisher, whether the whole or part of the material is concerned, specifically the rights of translation, reprinting, reuse of illustrations, recitation, broadcasting, reproduction on microfilms or in any other physical way, and transmission or information storage and retrieval, electronic adaptation, computer software, or by similar or dissimilar methodology now known or hereafter developed.
The use of general descriptive names, registered names, trademarks, service marks, etc. in this publication does not imply, even in the absence of a specific statement, that such names are exempt from the relevant protective laws and regulations and therefore free for general use.
The publisher, the authors and the editors are safe to assume that the advice and information in this book are believed to be true and accurate at the date of publication. Neither the publisher nor the authors or the editors give a warranty, expressed or implied, with respect to the material contained herein or for any errors or omissions that may have been made. The publisher remains neutral with regard to jurisdictional claims in published maps and institutional affiliations.

This Springer imprint is published by the registered company Springer Nature Switzerland AG
The registered company address is: Gewerbestrasse 11, 6330 Cham, Switzerland

If disposing of this product, please recycle the paper.

Foreword

The 20th International Federated Conference on Distributed Computing Techniques (DisCoTec 2025) took place from 16th to 20th of June, 2025 at the Lille campus of *Arts et Métiers* (ENSAM) and was organised by the Research center in Computer Science, Signal and Automatic Control of Lille (CRIStAL) with the support from the University of Lille, the Inria Centre at the University of Lille, and the French National Centre for Scientific Research (CNRS).

The DisCoTec series is one of the major events sponsored by the International Federation for Information Processing (IFIP). It comprises three conferences:

- The IFIP WG6.1 International Conference on Coordination Models and Languages (COORDINATION)
- The IFIP WG6.1 International Conference on Distributed Applications and Interoperable Systems (DAIS)
- The IFIP WG6.1 International Conference on Formal Techniques for Distributed Objects, Components and Systems (FORTE)

Together, these conferences cover a broad spectrum of distributed computing subjects, ranging from theoretical foundations and formal description techniques to systems research issues. Following the established tradition and in addition to the individual sessions of each conference, the event comprised several plenary sessions gathering attendants from the three conferences. These included for joint invited speaker sessions, a joint session for the best papers from each of the three conferences, a session dedicated to gender parity and the role of women in science, an event dedicated to the young researchers, and a session dedicated to the demonstration of the artefacts created by the community.

The main three conferences were further complemented by five satellite events:

- the workshop "Components Operationally: Reversibility and System Engineering" (CORSE), in honour of Jean-Bernard Stefani on the occasion of his 65th birthday
- the 18th International Workshop on Interaction and Concurrency Experience (ICE 2025)
- the 1st International Workshop on Adaptable Cloud Architectures (WACA 2025)
- three invited tutorials—one from each main conference—showcasing outstanding tools of interest to the community
- a full-day tutorial presenting the ΔQSD design paradigm

I would like to thank the Program Committee chairs, the Artefact Evaluation chairs, and the organisers of all the events for their involvement and cooperation during the preparation of the conference, and the Steering Committee and Advisory Boards of DisCoTec and the three main conferences for their guidance and support. The organisation of DisCoTec 2025 was only possible thanks to the dedicated work of the Organising Committee, including Bas van den Heuvel and Matthew Alan Le Brun (Publicity chairs), Roberto Casadei (Artefact Evaluation coordinating co-chair), Larisa Safina (Satellite

Events chair), Imen Sayar and Manel Barkallah (Gender Parity / Women in Sciences cochairs), Adrien Luxey-Bitri (Young Researchers Forum chair), Alexandre Desquesne, Aissa Ainaoui and Isabelle Aslani (logistics and finances), as well as all the students who volunteered their time to help, particularly Nathan Leblond and Rémy Raes (Head of Student Volunteers). Many thanks to Arts et Métiers, and particularly to Rodolphe Sory, for providing the infrastructure to host the event. Finally, I would like to thank IFIP WG6.1, Springer's Lecture Notes in Computer Science team, the University of Lille, the Inria Centre at the University of Lille, and the CRIStAL laboratory for their support and sponsorship. EasyChair provided the reviewing platform, whereas CNRS has provided the registration and accounting infrastructure. Last but not least, thanks to the DisCoTec community—both speakers and attendees—for making it happen.

Happy 20th anniversary, DisCoTec!

June 2025 Simon Bliudze

Preface

This volume contains the papers presented at DAIS 2025: the 25th International Conference on Distributed Applications and Interoperable Systems, sponsored by the International Federation for Information Processing (IFIP). The DAIS conference series addresses all practical and conceptual aspects of distributed applications, including their design, modeling, implementation, and operation; the supporting middleware; appropriate software engineering methodologies and tools; and experimental studies and applications. DAIS 2025 was held during June 16–20, 2025, in Lille, France, as part of DisCoTec 2025, the 20th International Federated Conference on Distributed Computing Techniques

We offered two distinct paper tracks: full research papers, and short papers. We received 16 submissions, where 15 were full papers and 1 was a short paper. All submissions were single-blind reviewed by at least three Program Committee (PC) members. The review process included a post-review discussion phase, during which the merits of all papers were discussed by the PC. The committee decided to accept five full research papers, for an acceptance rate of 31%. The accepted papers cover a broad range of topics in distributed computing: edge computing, data storage, data streaming, and mobile communication. The program also included one tutorial and one invited talk.

This year, we invited authors of accepted papers to submit publicly available artifacts associated with their papers. This process was chaired by Vinicius V. Cogo. We received 2 artifacts, which were each evaluated by four reviewers.

The keynotes for DAIS were presented by Alysson Bessani and Hélène Coullon. Alysson Bessani is currently an Associate Professor at the University of Lisbon Faculty of Sciences, Portugal. Hélène Coullon is currently an Associate Professor in computer science at IMT Atlantique, France.

The conference was made possible by the hard work and cooperation of many people working in several different committees and organizations, all of which are listed in these proceedings. In particular, we are grateful to the PC members for their commitment and thorough reviews, and for their active participation in the discussion phase, and to all the external reviewers for their help in evaluating submissions. Finally, we also thank the DisCoTec General Chair, Simon Bliudze, and the DAIS Steering Committee Chair, Luís Veiga, for their constant availability, support, and guidance.

June 2025

Daniel Balouek
Ibéria Medeiros

Organisation

Program Committee Chairs

Daniel Balouek   INRIA, France
Ibéria Medeiros   University of Lisbon, Portugal

Steering Committee

Lydia Y. Chen   TU Delft, Netherlands
Frank Eliassen   University of Oslo, Norway
Rüdiger Kapitza   Friedrich-Alexander-Universität
                               Erlangen-Nürnberg, Germany
Rui Oliveira   University of Minho / INESC TEC, Portugal
Hans P. Reiser   Reykjavik University, Iceland
Laura Ricci   University of Pisa, Italy
Silvia Bonomi   Università degli Studi di Roma "La Sapienza",
                               Italy
Etienne Riviére   Ecole Polytechnique de Louvain, Belgium
Jose Pereira   University of Minho / INESC TEC, Portugal
Luís Veiga   INESC-ID, Universidade de Lisboa, Portugal

Program Committee

Pierre-Louis Aublin   IIJ Research Laboratory, Japan
Daniel Balouek   INRIA, France
Christian Berger   University of Passau, Germany
David Bermbach   TU Berlin, Germany
Simon Bliudze   INRIA, France
Cláudia Brito   INESC TEC & U. Minho, Portugal
Lorenzo Carnevale   University of Messina, Italy
Zhiyuan Chen   University of Maryland Baltimore County, USA
Vinicius V. Cogo   Universidade de Lisboa, Portugal
Tânia Esteves   INESC TEC & U. Minho, Portugal
Giovanni Farina   Niccolò Cusano University, Italy
Davide Frey   INRIA, France
Pradeeban Kathiravelu   University of Alaska Anchorage, USA

João Leitão	Universidade Nova de Lisboa
Ibéria Medeiros	University of Lisbon, Portugal
Odorico M. Mendizabal	Universidade Federal de Santa Catarina, Brazil
Anas Mokhtari	IMT-Atlantique, France
Alan Oliveira de Sá	Universidade de Lisboa, Portugal
José Pedro Peixoto	INESC TEC & U. Minho, Portugal
Guillaume Pierre	University of Rennes, Inria, CNRS, IRISA, France
Rémy Raes	University of Lille, France
Hans P. Reiser	Reykjavik University, Iceland
Etienne Rivière	Université catholique de Louvain, Belgique
Guillaume Rosinosky	IMT Atlantique, CNRS, Inria, France
Valerio Schiavoni	University of Neuchâtel, Switzerland
Robin Vassantlal	Universidade de Lisboa, Portugal
Luis Veiga (chair)	INESC ID Lisboa, Instituto Superior Técnico, Universidade de Lisboa, Portugal
Spyros Voulgaris	Vrije Universiteit Amsterdam, The Netherlands

Artefact Evaluation Chairs

Alan Oliveira de Sá	LASIGE & Faculdade de Ciências, Universidade de Lisboa, Portugal
Cláudia Brito	INESC TEC & U. Minho, Portugal
Christian Berger	University of Passau, Germany
Giovanni Farina	Niccolò Cusano University, Italy
José Pedro Peixoto	INESC TEC & U. Minho, Portugal
Rémy Raes	University of Lille, France
Robin Vassantlal	LASIGE & Faculdade de Ciências, Universidade de Lisboa, Portugal
Tânia Esteves	INESC TEC & U. Minho, Portugal
Vinícius V. Cogo (chair)	LASIGE & Faculdade de Ciências, Universidade de Lisboa, Portugal

Contents

A Critical Review of Mobile Device-to-Device Communication 1
   Lauric Desauw, Adrien Luxey-Bitri, Rémy Raes, Romain Rouvoy,
   Olivier Ruas, and Walter Rudametkin

Multi-provider Capabilities in EnOSlib: Driving Distributed System
Experiments on the Edge-to-Cloud Continuum 25
   Baptiste Jonglez, Matthieu Simonin, Jolan Philippe,
   and Sidi Mohammed Kaddour

Mitigating Cryptographic Bottlenecks of Low-Latency BFT Protocols 43
   Pierre-Louis Aublin and Arne Vogel

BCProf: Battery Consumption Profiler for Android Applications 64
   Lyla Naghipour Vijouyeh, Luís Veiga, and Paulo Ferreira

GT-LSTM: Integrating High-Resolution Particulate Matter Data for Urban
Air Quality Forecasting 84
   Maryam Rahmani, Suzanne Crumeyrolle, Nadège Martiny,
   and Romain Rouvoy

Justin: Hybrid CPU/Memory Elastic Scaling for Distributed Stream
Processing 102
   Donatien Schmitz, Guillaume Rosinosky, and Etienne Rivière

AIõRT: AI-Driven Distributed System for Heterogenous Internet
of Robotic Things in Sustainable Ecosystem 119
   Hanyue Xu, Yuanxin Su, Kah Phooi Seng, Chenghao Li, Han Lu,
   Jianfei He, and Li-Minn Ang

Author Index 131

A Critical Review of Mobile Device-to-Device Communication

Lauric Desauw[1], Adrien Luxey-Bitri[1]($\boxtimes$)[iD], Rémy Raes[1][iD], Romain Rouvoy[1][iD], Olivier Ruas[2][iD], and Walter Rudametkin[3][iD]

[1] Univ. Lille, Inria, CNRS, UMR 9189 CRIStAL, Lille, France
`lauric@deuxfleurs.fr`, `{adrien.luxey,remy.raes,romain.rouvoy}@inria.fr`
[2] Pathway, Paris, France
`olivier@pathway.com`
[3] Univ. Rennes, CNRS, Inria, IRISA, IUF, Rennes, France
`walter.rudametkin@inria.fr`

Abstract. Since the advent of mobile devices, both end-users and the IT industry have been longing for direct *device-to-device* (D2D) communication capabilities, expecting new kinds of interactive, personalized, and collaborative services. Fifteen years later, many D2D solutions have been implemented and deployed, but their availability and functionality are underwhelming. Arguably, the most widely-adopted D2D use case covers the pairing of accessories with smartphones; however, many other use cases—such as mobile media sharing—did not progress. Pervasive computing and cyber-physical convergence need local communication paradigms to scale. For inherently local use cases, they are even more appealing than ever: eschewing third-parties simultaneously fosters environmental sustainability, privacy, and network resiliency. This paper proposes a survey on D2D communication, investigates its deployment and adoption, with the objective of easing the creation and adoption of modern D2D frameworks. We present the results of an online poll that estimates end-users' utilization of D2D processes and review enabling technologies and security models.

1 Introduction

Device-to-device (D2D) communication refers to the capability of mobile devices to communicate directly with one another, eschewing intermediaries, such as a cellular base station. The D2D paradigm has been physically enabled for a long time by a wide range of wireless communication channels (e.g. infrared, Wi-Fi, Bluetooth, NFC, UWB), but it failed to be largely adopted by user-facing applications. It is currently hindered by technical (and non-technical) barriers that make it an unsuitable choice for developers and end-users alike. Most networked applications thus rely on centralized infrastructures, even for inherently local use cases, such as proximity sensing and face-to-face media exchanges—which limits the capacity of pervasive cyber-physical systems to scale [25,26]. D2D communication would have an important part to play in modern communication, however: due to its low infrastructural environmental footprint, inherent privacy, and for the pathway it paves to pervasive services beyond the Internet. This article thus proposes a critical survey of D2D's state of the art, focused on gathering insights to further its appropriation by the community. *What is the current deployment and adoption status of the device-to-device stack, what are its capabilities, and how can it be leveraged on widely available commodity hardware?* To answer these questions, we will report on: *(i)* the results of an online poll on D2D usage conducted by our team, featuring 364 participants; *(ii)* a review of the D2D communication channels that are the most widely available to end-users; *(iii)* an analysis of the D2D's paradigm security model.

1.1 Scope

'Device-to-device communication' is an umbrella term that has many definitions. In this article, we frame a definition of D2D focused on user-centric use cases. We consider a D2D communication as an exchange of information that happens *wirelessly*, in a *single hop* (without intermediaries), using channels and protocols already available on commodity *end-user mobile devices*. Intermediaries, such as a cellular base station, might assist in the establishment of the connection, but should not participate beyond that. This article does not cover *machine-to-machine* (M2M) applications, although some M2M-oriented protocols will be presented. Indeed, automatic communication between machines is not user-centric, and generally does not leverage the same protocols as the ones available on end-user equipment.

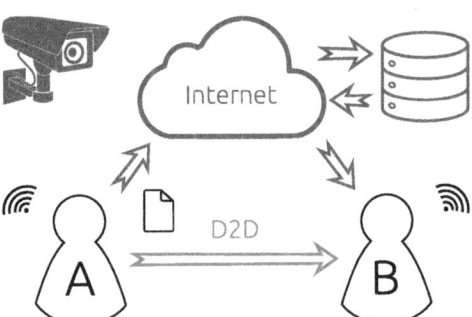

Fig. 1. For an inherently D2D use case such as transferring a file between nearby users, resorting to an Internet service for the exchange leads to more energy consumption, more storage space used, and exposes the users to digital surveillance (degraded privacy).

1.2 D2D Scenarios

Jameel *et al.* [50] proposed a taxonomy of D2D use cases, namely traffic offloading, providing emergency services, extending cellular coverage, reliable health monitoring, mobile tracking and positioning, and data dissemination. Among these use cases, we do not address provisioning emergency services, as it leverages multi-hop communication through advanced routing. Health monitoring and mobile tracking are left aside, because they utilize specialized sensor networks outside the end-users' realm (e.g. M2M communication). Traffic offloading and extension of cellular coverage revolve around facilitating access to Internet services, and are thus not our focus—although they will be mentioned. Finally, our paper specifically targets *user-centric data dissemination*, from direct file sharing to collaborative social services, such as crowdsourced environment sensing. An example of the file-sharing scenario is given in Fig. 1 where, in contrast to the use of Internet services, two users who share a file directly achieve better energy efficiency, less resource consumption and better privacy (cf. Sect. 2). Our online survey, presented in Sect. 3, shows that participants face this use case on a regular basis.

This rest of this paper is organised as follows: Sect. 2 first motivates the need for D2D communication. In Sect. 3, we report on an online poll that was conducted by our team on D2D usage, and analyse its results. Section 4 then describes the physical channels enabling D2D communication, while Sect. 5 presents the D2D security model and its properties. Section 6 finally discusses our findings and concludes this paper.

2 Motivation

Networked user applications are thriving, and Internet traffic is growing at an astonishing rate.[1] Yet, nearly all users' network sessions transit through the *cloud*: a cohort of data centers that feature high-grade equipments and are physically connected as close as possible to the Internet's 'backbone'. In this section, we develop several arguments that advocate for more D2D communications in mobile device networking.

2.1 Supporting the Energy Transitions

We first consider the example depicted in Fig. 1, where Alice and Bob, who are physically close, want to share a file. Unless both users own Apple products that feature AirDrop, as of now, the typical 'netizen' will adopt an indirect solution by uploading files to an online service (e.g. file storage, e-mail, instant communication) before their recipient can fetch them. The alternative is more direct and leverages a D2D protocol (e.g. Bluetooth, Wi-Fi Direct), such that the file is immediately transmitted from Alice's smartphone to Bob's, without the intervention of any intermediaries. How is the indirect solution more costly? To answer, we need to break down a online-based file exchange: Alice's file needs to be transmitted from her smartphone to her network gateway (either her Wi-Fi access point or her cellular base station), and further transmitted over the

---

[1] See Cisco's Annual Internet Reports [24] and Wikipedia's 'Internet Traffic' page for aggregated data [91].

Internet to the data centre where the online service will store the file on a persistent storage. Then, Bob needs to connect to the same service, so the file performs approximately the same journey back from the data centre's storage, over the Internet to Bob's network gateway, and to Bob's smartphone. This *sharing-as-a-service* process supported by the cloud is costly in several regards:

- *Data in transit*: On its way to & from the data centre, the file hops through an unbounded amount of network equipments (routers, switches, cables). Although the electrical consumption and related carbon footprint of data in transfer are hard to measure and individually negligible, this typical use case—globally—induces a non-negligible load on the network [65], leading to the necessity to keep increasing and maintaining the Internet's throughput;
- *Network congestion*: Increasing the Internet's throughput imposes to build more infrastructures, producing more routers and cables, consuming more electricity, and consequently extracting more raw materials from the Earth [43];
- *Cold storage*: The third-party server has to store a copy of the file that could remain there for an unknown time [23]. The service provider thus requires an ever-increasing storage capacity (e.g., hard drives) to sustain their customers' demands.

By shifting direct communication between user devices, the aforementioned costs would be highly limited. Only the incompressible energy and storage required to locally transfer the file between the two devices would be consumed. In essence, to lower the environmental impact of the Internet, it is crucial to shorten communication chains, wherever possible. We postulate that—given the digitalization of our lives and the variety of use cases that could eschew a cloud third-party—the raw material savings enabled by D2D communication are substantial, thanks to its lower electrical consumption and negligible use of infrastructure.

2.2 Unplugging the Surveillance Economy

Every time Alice makes a connection or *request* to a data center to use an online service, the following actors obtain details of the communication:

- The network operators (notably Alice's *Internet Service Provider* (ISP) or cellular network provider), as well as the data centre's owner, obtain Alice's IP address, the potentially encrypted payload, its size, and the request timestamp. If the connection is not encrypted, they can also read the request's content. Even when encryption is enforced, a more intrusive operator may also be able to obtain information about Alice's device or to inspect the content of her requests—for example through *Deep Packet Inspection* (DPI) [10];
- In addition to the above, the cloud service operator obtains application-specific information, as well as the payload of the request. Following our file sharing use case, the cloud service obtains the filename, size, content, and likely the recipient's address or identifier (e.g. their e-mail address).

Network service providers are legally bound to retain this data for security purposes [28]. Besides this legal requirement, Shoshana Zuboff [93] describes how the digital economy revolves around the accumulation and processing of personal data for financial benefit. Although each datum is seemingly harmless, this 'surveillance economy' poses serious threats to individuals [4], free speech [60], and democratic societies at large [21,55,56]. By eschewing third parties, D2D communication holds great potential to prevent the accumulation and marketization of personal information and its detrimental effects.

2.3 Uneven Access to a Broadband Internet Connection

Worldwide, access to the Internet and to mobile devices is highly uneven: in 2021 almost half of the World's population is kept offline, according to the United Nations [81]. Surprisingly, 94% of people are within coverage of a mobile broadband network [33]. In addition to the half billion people without coverage, billions more who could have access cannot afford it. The geographical distribution of people without access to the Internet shows that Africa is the continent of most concern [44], but there are local disparities within many countries [83].

People's budgets may be the main cause of this digital divide. Indeed, users need to buy a device and, arguably more importantly, they must pay service fees to access the Internet. Prices vary widely per country and depend on many factors. The impact on consumers also depends on their purchasing power. And, while unlimited data plans do exist, most people still pay per gigabyte consumed or have limited plans. In 2022, comparing China to the United States shows a 6.4 times difference in pricing, with average prices of $0.41 and $5.62 USD per GB of mobile data, respectively [20]. However, countries with very similar culture and purchasing power can also have very different data rates, as shown through France and Belgium, two neighbouring European countries. In 2021, France had a median price per GB of $0.41 USD, while in Belgium the median price was $5.28 USD/GB: 12.8 times more expensive. As data usage increases due to the growing volumes of content (such as video streaming), connection fees can be a burden to many, including in developed countries, such as the U.S. [57]. By enabling proximity networking without fees, D2D communication would be a way to decrease those costs and to include the discarded of the digital divide. Local communications can also provide basic connectivity in situations where Internet coverage is unavailable or inconsistent (e.g. in planes, inside buildings or in disaster situations).

3 The Discouraging D2D User Experience

We conducted an online survey on 'how people usually share documents between physically close devices', available at https://d2dsurvey.luxeylab.net. along with the survey answers' raw data. This use case could typically be undertaken using D2D protocols. Our goal was to estimate how the public achieves it, and their satisfaction using the different solutions available. After a short inquiry of their

IT know-how, participants were asked about the frequency with which they need to exchange documents between nearby devices. Then, they were asked to express how often they use, and their level of satisfaction with regard to Bluetooth, external storage (ext), cloud services, and lastly AirDrop for Apple users only. A free-text field allowed participants to provide comments and feedback. We gathered 364 answers, including 64% professionals of the IT community.

There is a Need for D2D Communication. Figure 2 shows the distribution of the frequency of the need to share files between nearby devices. 61% of the participants face the use case weekly or more, while only 12% need D2D file sharing less than once a month. This figure highlights the ubiquity of media exchange in our digital lifestyles: from lolcats and memes, to text documents (administrative, press...), including voice recordings, souvenir pictures and videos, etc.

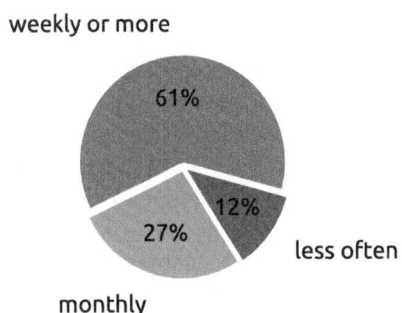

Fig. 2. Distribution of the frequency of the need for D2D communication. 61% of the surveyed users need D2D communication at least once a week, while only 12% need it less than once a month.

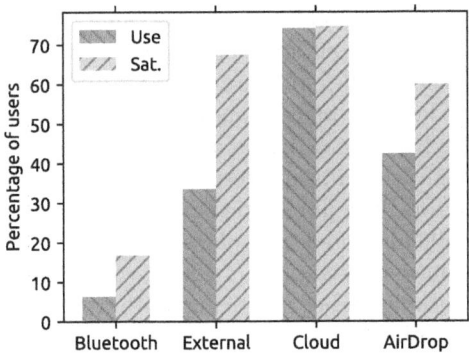

Fig. 4. Use and satisfaction (Sat.) of the different available technologies. For the use, only users frequently using the given technology are taken into account. Bluetooth is the least popular technology to exchange documents between nearby devices, despite being designed for this purpose. On the other hand, the cloud is the preferred solution, while it is the only not relying on the device proximity.

Fig. 3. Alternate solutions used by participants of our survey for close file sharing, proposed in the free-text field. Technologies are not exclusive, e.g. *Samba* is generally a *Windows Local net* solution. Font-size is proportional to the proposition's frequency.

Many Alternate Solutions to a Simple Problem. Out of the 364 participants, 82 left an answer in the free-text feedback field. As shown in Fig. 3, people solve the close file sharing issue within their entourage using many alternate solutions: D2D or not, ad-hoc or purposeful. Notably: Syncthing[2], Samba, sharedrop.io, KDE Connect, Warpinator, proximity sharing with a Wi-Fi Hotspot (Local net), rsync (CLI), etc. This variety can be interpreted in different ways. On the one hand, it shows the versatility of the digital tool, as it enables many different ways to solve a simple task. On the other hand, it also highlights the lack of a universal D2D solution for file exchange.

Existing D2D Technologies are not Satisfactory. Fig. 4 reports on the percentage of participants who frequently use each technology and their level of satisfaction. Except for AirDrop, the satisfaction percentages are computed on the total number of participants and not only on those frequently using the given technology, since not being satisfied about a technology has an impact on its usage frequency. For AirDrop, the percentages are computed only for Apple users.

Only 6% use Bluetooth frequently, and only 17% are satisfied with it. While AirDrop seems to be a better D2D alternative for Mac users, 42% of Mac users use it frequently and 60% deem it satisfactory. Non-D2D technologies are significantly preferred. 34% of the participants frequently use external storage, with 67% satisfaction. The most frequently used technology to exchange documents between nearby devices is, ironically, the cloud: 74% of the participants frequently use it for that purpose, and 75% are satisfied with it.

A first observation is that, despite the need for D2D file sharing, people rarely use Bluetooth or Airdrop. They prefer other sharing means (external storage, or mostly the cloud). Airdrop has a usage and a satisfaction percentage of 42% and 60% respectively, among Apple-using participants. Both statistics fall below that of the cloud. The lack of inter-compatibility with other vendors may partly explain this underwhelming observation. However, the real question lies in the minor 17% satisfaction towards Bluetooth, and its even lower 6% usage rate. This disuse is surprising, given that this channel is notably built for the very purpose of exchanging files. Regarding external storage, its 34% usage rate can be explained by the burden of using a storage proxy, including cables. However, participants are fairly satisfied with it: once plugged in, cabled solutions are indeed reliable. Finally, regarding the cloud: its 75% satisfaction rate is in line with the amount of investment and the many actors involved in network-based file exchange. However, following our paper's motivation, we deem that 74% *of the participants regularly resorting to the cloud for such a D2D scenario is bad news*. For the sake of the environmental footprint of ICT, privacy and users' data bills, professionals ought to work towards reducing this proportion in favour of D2D channels. The rest of this article presents communication channels and security models to this end.

---

[2] Syncthing exists precisely to allow file exchange without involving third-parties. It works over the Internet, or in a D2D fashion if the involved devices share a local network. See https://syncthing.net/.

4 Communication Channels

The *radio frequency* (RF) spectrum is regulated in every country: it is forbidden to emit on specific frequency bands without authorisation. Consequently, each RF channel resides on an agreed-upon frequency band. In the first subsection, we introduce the D2D channels existing in radio bands that are free to use without authorisation, called *unlicensed* or *out-band* frequency bands. In Subsect. 4.2, we turn our attention to D2D communication channels that make use of *licensed* cellular networks, hence requiring a subscription. Subsection 4.3 then presents several proprietary solutions that leverage upon physical channels in order to provide user-friendly D2D connectivity. Finally, Subsect. 4.4 explains how all these channels are made available to the users on the hardware level.

Table 1 features a compilation of communication channels that were considered the most readily available for D2D applications to this day—interestingly, all of them are out-band. Channels are arranged in families, either because they employ similar spectrum, or because they emanate from the same family of standards. For each standards' family, several specifications were displayed to show the evolution of their characteristics, as specification efforts progressed.

4.1 Out-Band Channels

Free-Space Optical Communication (FSO). Free-space optical communication has been used by humanity since its infancy—from smoke signals, to optical telegraphs, and the most recent visual light communication technologies.

Infrared Communication. Infrared refers to the electromagnetic spectrum between 300 GHz and 430 THz (visible red light), and was first 'discovered' in 1800 by astronomer Herschel [67]. Since then, it has found countless applications, from night vision to astronomy to communication. As a consumer product, infrared is routinely used for e.g. televisions' remote control. Nintendo featured infrared sensors in most of their gaming consoles: from the 1998's GameBoy Color up to the 2017's Switch [63]. It seems, however, that only a few games ever made use of the feature, highlighting a developers' preference for other wireless communication channels. Nevertheless, to this day, several smartphone manufacturers continue to ship infrared 'blasters' in their products, Xiaomi notably provides a TV remote control application leveraging their smartphones' infrared sensors [92]. Infrared communication requires that the emitter and receiver be in direct line of sight. Depending on the source intensity, the maximum communication distance can span miles. Most of infrared's commercial applications employ proprietary protocols, although the *Infrared Data Association* (IrDA) provides a standard protocol since 1994 [42], advertising a data rate of up to 16 Mb/s.

Table 1. Characteristics of the most widely available D2D communication channels

Name	Specification date	Device discovery*	Maximum distance**	Maximum data rate	Frequency
Optical					
Infrared (IrDA)	1994[42]	Manual	Several meters	16 Mb/s	0.3–430 THz
QRCode-flashing	—	Manual	Around a meter	23.6 kb/picture	440-790 THz
Wi-Fi					
802.11 (legacy)	1997[35]	Automatic	100 m	1–2 Mb/s	2.4 GHz
802.11ax (Wi-Fi 6E)	2021[39]	Automatic	100 m	1.2 Gb/s	1–7.125 GHz
802.11ay	2021[40]	Automatic	10 m	100 Gb/s	60 GHz
Bluetooth					
Bluetooth Core v1	1999[14]	Automatic	100 m	1 Mb/s	2.4 GHz
Bluetooth Core v5	2016[16]	Automatic	100 m	1–3 Mb/s[17]	2.4 GHz
RFID					
NFC	2004[46]	Manual	20 cm	106–424 kb/s	13.56 MHz
Ultra-WideBand					
UWB	2007[47,48]	Automatic	200 m	27 Mb/s	3.1–10.6 GHz

* Some channels require *manual* human supervision to be used, whereas some others *automatically* discover peers in the vicinity.
** The range of a radio signal depends on its frequency (which drives signal attenuation) and on the antenna's power and type (directional or omni-directional), not on its underlying standard [19]. The maximum distances presented here refer to typical user equipment.

QRCode-flashing Recent years have seen the advent of a one-way D2D communication channel—so ubiquitous it does not even have a name: shooting a QR code from a device's screen to another device through its camera. The practice arises from QR codes, a well-settled technology that has already found worldwide adoption. As a replacement to lower-capacity barcodes, QR codes are routinely used for product tracing, loyalty programs and the like. It enables augmented reality applications, to display restaurants' menus or to locate objects in a 3D space. Finally, in recent years, the QRCode-flashing channel has found massive public adoption, as it is pervasively used as an authentication technique for, e.g., travel tickets, Wi-Fi log-in and, most recently, Covid-19 contact tracing and access control [61]. According to its ISO specification [49], a QR code is capable of holding up to 23.6 kb of data—depending on the code's size, data type, and level of *Error Correction Coding* (ECC). Specifically, as a means to transfer information from a screen-enabled device to a camera-enabled one, it intuitively sounds impractical to use the QRCode-flashing D2D channel as a data streaming interface. Indeed, generating, capturing and interpreting a QR code is somehow cumbersome and time-intensive. For the time being, let us only consider the channel as a means to exchange one-way *pulses* of data.

Wi-Fi. In 1996, Chai-Keong Toh deposited a patent for routing ad hoc mobile networks, published in 1999 [79]. In 1997, the IEEE 802.11 Working Group published its first standard for wireless network communication in the 2.4 GHz frequency band [35], inside which the 'ad hoc network' mode was a first-class citizen. Considered as 'beta', this initial standard was superseded in 1999 by 802.11a [36] and 802.11b [37], which found a massive adoption by manufacturers, and finally allowed 'Wi-Fi' to become the ubiquitous wireless medium that we know.

'Ad hoc networking' enables direct communication between end-devices, that is D2D communication. Additionally, it supports multi-hop routing: two out-of-range devices can communicate through Wi-Fi ad hoc by using an intermediary gateway device, effectively enabling *Mobile Ad hoc Networks* (MANETs) [27]— which is outside the scope of this article. Lastly, Wi-Fi ad hoc features the mesh topology, where any two devices connected to a Wi-Fi ad hoc network can directly communicate with one another, without going through the gateway node, as long as they are in range. It is notable that D2D communication was seriously considered by pioneers of Wi-Fi from its inception, and even beforehand. Wireless network card manufacturers did implement the functionality, resulting in academic experiments on ad hoc networks from 2000 onwards, notably by the aforementioned patent holder C.-K. Toh [77, 78]. Because 'Wi-Fi ad hoc' exists since Wi-Fi's inception, it features the same capabilities as the most recent Wi-Fi standards' implementations: as of 2021, the information rate climbs up to 20 Gb/s at close range using the 60 GHz band (standard 802.11ay [40]), while it maxes out at 9, 608 Mb/s on the traditional 4.2–6 GHz band (standard 802.11ax, also called Wi-Fi 6E [39]). Concurrently to IEEE 802.11's standardization efforts, the Wi-Fi Alliance periodically proposes standards enabling new applications and improved user experience with Wi-Fi.

Wi-Fi Direct. 'Wi-Fi Direct' [87] (formerly 'Wi-Fi P2P') was introduced in 2010 by the Wi-Fi Alliance, in an initiative to make ad hoc networks simpler. This specification makes Wi-Fi operations closer to Bluetooth for use cases like device pairing, with the superior bandwidths of the Wi-Fi family. Wi-Fi Direct restricts itself to single-hop communication in a star topology (all communications go through the Wi-Fi Direct gateway, coined the Group Owner). By re-using Wi-Fi features from previous norms, only one of the Wi-Fi devices needs to be compliant with Wi-Fi Direct.

Wi-Fi Aware. 'Wi-Fi Aware' [89] was introduced in 2015, mostly as a tool aggregating Wi-Fi and *Bluetooth Low Energy* (BLE) to deliver energy-efficient advertisement & discovery of services in proximity. Users can read insightful data from 'beaconing' devices (i.e. devices only emitting short pulses of information) without connecting to them, although the specification also allows switching to a connected mode arranged in a mesh topology (no group owner). The Android kernel supports Wi-Fi Aware since 2017 [32], hinting that the technology might have been considered by Google as a beaconing back-end. However, no other OS supports Wi-Fi Aware, effectively making it an Android-specific artefact.

Bluetooth (BT). Bluetooth is another ubiquitous wireless communication channel utilizing the unlicensed 2.4 GHz radio band. Following its first specification by the Bluetooth *Special Interest Group* (SIG) in 1999 [14], the first Bluetooth-enabled consumer device was a hands-free headset, highlighting BT's core objective: to obsolete cables for connecting digital peripherals—a typical D2D use case. At the time of writing, Bluetooth 5.4, published in February 2023, is the latest of 14 *core* specifications of the protocol [17, 18]. BT standards are split into tens of *profiles* [90], segregated per usage scenario. Profiles are not necessarily tied to a specific core specification. Each BT-enabled device only needs to support a subset of the available profiles—e.g. '*Advanced Audio Distribution Profile* (A2DP)' for a wireless headset—facilitating Bluetooth implementation for device manufacturers. BT creates point-to-point connections, called *pairs*, having a primary/secondary relationship. Bluetooth connections support up to 1–3 Mb/s date rates. A primary device can concurrently maintain connections with up to seven secondary nodes, resulting in a star-topology network coined a 'piconet' [68].

Bluetooth Low Energy (BLE). BLE is a protocol stack that allows BT to operate on small-size devices with very low power requirements (0.01–0.50 W). It enabled the cheap manufacture of 'beacons': small devices only used for broadcasting small bursts of information (they never create a full connection). This class of small-scale devices opened the door to new use cases, such as indoor geolocation (where BLE beacons are scattered in an indoor location to allow Bluetooth-enabled devices to locate themselves). BLE being a different protocol from 'classical Bluetooth', they are incompatible. However, most appliances supporting the latter (e.g. smartphones) are 'dual-mode': they also implement the BLE protocol.

Bluetooth and Wi-Fi may appear to be competing for the wireless consumer market: Wi-Fi supports much higher data rates, while BT's profiles make the latter cheaper and more straightforward to implement on low-end IoT devices. However, several proposals leverage both channels (e.g. Wi-Fi Aware), which hints that they might just as well be used in combination to improve the overall D2D connectivity.

Radio-Frequency IDentification (RFID). Operating on MHz bands with a data rate in the order of kb/s, RFID is a particularly cheap short-range wireless channel. It has been commercially deployed for decades as a remote identification technology for, e.g., theft prevention, goods inventories & access-control through badges [13]. This is thanks to RFID 'tags', which are able to emit beacons using only the RF energy harvested from their environment, without a battery [85, 86]. In 2004, the ISO standardised NFC [46], a novel communication protocol based on RFID. Most modern smartphones nowadays fully support NFC. Operating at 13.56 MHz with a maximum throughput of 424 kb/s, NFC allows contactless communication between devices over a few centimetres. This short range requires little power, and eschews interference issues. Due to its low throughput, NFC is a bad fit for demanding data exchanges. However, it is a very compelling channel for secure authentication, as emphasized by its broad adoption for contact-less payment and the newest Wi-Fi authentication schemes (see Sect. 5.3).

Ultra-WideBand (UWB). UWB is characterized by its wide frequency band (500 MHz). It transmits several bits of information in one *pulse*, over a range of frequencies. This operating mode differentiates it from most other wireless channels, that exchange a bit per time step over a single frequency. Despite being one of the first radio communication channels, UWB was only granted an authorization for commercial use by the FCC in 2002, on the unlicensed 3.1–10.6 GHz frequency band [64,72]. The ISO publishes UWB standards since 2007 [47,48]. It is sponsored by the UWB Alliance and the FiRa Consortium since 2019. IEEE's working group 802.15 on *Wireless Personal Area Networks* (WPANs) is working towards a specification since 2020. Deployment-wise, the iPhone 11 (2019) was the first consumer mobile device to support UWB [9], thanks to Apple's U1 chip (see Sect. 4.4).

As a D2D communication channel, UWB is advertised as a low-energy, high-throughput (27 Mb/s) channel supporting a range of several hundred meters. It is also expected to become a precise geo-location and tracking technology [72].

Discarded Channels. According to our definition of D2D communication, Zig-Bee [38], Li-Fi [45], LoRa [11] and SigFox [52] are outside the scope of this article: they require dedicated hardware that is not widely available on consumer mobile devices. Some of these protocols additionally require a third-party coordinator to exchange data between two peers. Nevertheless, they are worth considering in broader D2D studies for several reasons: Li-Fi eschews radio interferences by working on the visible light spectrum; the *Low Power Wide Area Network* (LPWAN) properties of LoRa & SigFox are particularly interesting for the IoT sector [58] and geo-location [3]; and ZigBee—intended to be a simpler protocol than BT & Wi-Fi—can be a good fit on low-end embedded devices (e.g. sensors).

4.2 In-Band Channels

Cellular communication is regulated by the global standards organization 3GPP (for '3rd Generation Partnership Project'). The 3GPP began working on D2D communication in 2011, as part of their Release 12 (or Rel12) [1], which was frozen in 2015. The focus was put on public safety & critical communication sectors (as a replacement for the legacy Land Mobile Radio channel or LMR), resulting in two 3GPP 'Work Items': *Proximity Services* (ProSe), and Group Communication. The integration of emerging D2D use cases in further 3GPP releases continues as time passes. The latest frozen release, Rel15 [2] notably took interest in *Internet of Things* (IoT), *Machine Type Communication* (MTC) and *Vehicle-to-Everything* (V2x) use cases. Although 3GPP protocols, such as *LTE for Machines* (LTE-M) and *NarrowBand-IoT* (NB-IoT), support direct communication between devices (without going through any cellular base station) [50,51], hardware support seems entirely absent from end-user appliances.

4.3 Proprietary Solutions

Specialized devices typically feature ad-hoc wireless communication protocols, although generally not available on mainstream end-user equipment. An iconic example is Apple, which is well-known for streamlining their users' experience across devices (e.g. iPhone, iMac, Apple TV...) through proprietary protocols. Particularly interesting in the context of D2D communication are the AirPlay & AirDrop services, due to their wide adoption and acknowledged performance (as observed in Sect. 3). AirPlay [6], dating back to 2004, only specialises in streaming audiovisual content from computers (including phones and tablets) to TVs and speakers. AirDrop, on the other hand, is a general purpose file transfer solution. It was initially released in 2011, and can only be used between Apple devices. Both services are backed by the undocumented, proprietary *Apple Wireless Direct Link* (AWDL) protocol, and leverage standard close-range wireless channels: Wi-Fi & Bluetooth, and UWB since iPhone 11 [72]. The *Open Wireless Link* (OWL) project [74] has been reverse-engineering AWDL since 2018 [73]. The OWL project's continued work include the publication of security flaws inside AWDL [75] and an open implementation of AirDrop, coined OpenDrop [69].

Since 2018, Google also proposes a proprietary D2D solution for Android phones, entitled *Google Nearby Connections* (GNC) [31]. As part of the Android Play Services, it is therefore installed in most Android phones. Contrarily to AirDrop, GNC exposes APIs to application developers, allowing any Android app to establish general-purpose direct connections between phones (and even groups of phones). Antonioli *et al.* [5] reverse-engineered GNC in 2019, exposing severe security breaches in the same paper. The paper shows that GNC operates similarly to AWDL.

Because they are undocumented and only leverage standard channels, AirDrop and GNC were left-out from Table 1. However, these two proprietary channels still demonstrate that performant and reliable D2D communication is feasible, and mostly seems to demand a concerned OS support.

4.4 Hardware

General Case. Since 2007's iPhone 1 [8], smartphones have always supported at least cellular network, Wi-Fi, and Bluetooth communication. At the time, mobile phones used to contain one chip per channel. Nowadays however, most mobile phones contain a single circuit chip (a *System on a Chip* or SoC) that integrates most of the features needed for a smartphone—i.e. CPU, GPU, volatile memory, network connectivity, camera... One of the most widely deployed SoC as of 2023 is the SnapDragon series from Qualcomm that supports Bluetooth, Wi-Fi, cellular, and NFC communication. Another one is the Dimensity series by MediaTek, featuring the same connectivity support. Since 2021, Google designs its own SoC, coined Tensor, which is shipped inside the Google Pixel series of smartphones, from version 6 onwards [62]. Guessing from a system parameter to disable UWB on Pixel 6 Pro [53], the Tensor SoC supports UWB additionally to the above-mentioned channels. Lastly, some SoC with no connectivity support also exist, such as the Kirin by HiSilicon. Smartphones equipped with the latter host additional hardware for wireless communication.

In the end, all smartphones support Wi-Fi and Bluetooth, the most ubiquitous out-band channels for D2D communication. Hardware support for UWB is still nascent. None of the current SoC for smartphones support in-band channels, such as LTE-M or NB-IoT (cf. Sect. 4.2), nor atypical channels like ZigBee (Sect. 4.1).

The Special Case of Apple. Apple devices are now fully designed by Apple: from the hardware, to the OS, to the system APIs. Nevertheless, Apple's developments are generally closed-source, making it hard for the most curious of us to scrutinize their products' operations. As presented in Sect. 4.3, Apple's AirPlay and AirDrop D2D protocols are backed by the (AWDL) D2D protocol, which functions atop standard Wi-Fi chips according to the OWL project [73,74]. Since 2019, iPhones are packaged with the U1 network chip [7], which additionally supports the *Ultra-WideBand* (UWB) channel [12].

5 Security Models

Compared to the Internet, the unique properties of D2D communication impose specific security challenges. On one hand, D2D locality obviates most remote attack scenarios, which are daunting in the Internet paradigm. On the other hand, the broadcast nature of D2D wireless channels and the need for periodic self-advertisement introduce new classes of attacks. This section overviews the security model of D2D communication. Several surveys propose a more in-depth study [34,84]. Section 5.1 introduces D2D attack scenarios, before enumerating desired security properties. Section 5.3 presents D2D-specific security features. Finally, as an example of these features, we briefly describe Bluetooth and Wi-Fi current authentication schemes in Sect. 5.4.

5.1 Attack Scenarios

Passive Attacks. Due to the broadcast nature of wireless communication, an adversary *in the vicinity of a user* may passively eavesdrop and/or analyse D2D traffic to learn sensitive information about other peers.

Unencrypted messages are directly accessible through *eavesdropping*, while *traffic analysis* can infer context information, even on encrypted traffic, such as the object of a transmission (text, file, stream...) or the service being used. Location information can also be passively inferred, such as D2D users' whereabouts and travel patterns [66].

Active Attacks. An active adversary may perform a *Denial of Service* (DoS) attack by *jamming* the communication medium. By *forging* and/or *manipulating* D2D messages, a malicious user in transmission range can further trick honest peers: they may access unauthorized services, impersonate the identity of other persons, or even steal information from their victims.

5.2 Desired Security and Privacy Properties

D2D security as a whole is driven by network security & privacy requirements. The two concepts are very interrelated, although they sometimes conflict.

Network Security. The three usual tenets of network security are: **availability**, the fact of ensuring that the network is always accessible; **integrity**, which protects users against the modification or falsification of exchanged information; and **confidentiality**, ensuring that only authorized users can read a piece of information [70]. This latter is enabled by *cryptographic authentication*, which provides for both *identification* and *encryption* [71]. Encryption is of paramount importance in wireless, as any eavesdropper in range can read unencrypted traffic.

Privacy. Privacy does not hold any widely accepted definition, but can be defined as a personal decision to define which personal information one agrees to share with whom, how, and to what extent. There is an inherent trade-off between privacy and utility, as the utility of a service generally increases as it is provided with more personal information on its user [34]. In D2D communication, the major pillars of network privacy are: **user anonymity**, or hiding from unauthorized peers any information that could be used to find one's identity; **context privacy**, which prevents attackers from learning context information about a communication (e.g., location, service being used, query type); and **unlinkability**, that aims at making several communication sessions by the same user indistinguishable from sessions by different users (one's communication history cannot be *linked*). As opposed to user anonymity—that takes interest in the messages' *content*, unlinkability takes interest in the *way* messages are sent [54].

5.3 D2D-Specific Security Features

Figure 5 depicts how D2D-specific features enable the aforementioned security properties. We focus on network security properties, and not privacy ones, as the former knows more consensual definitions.

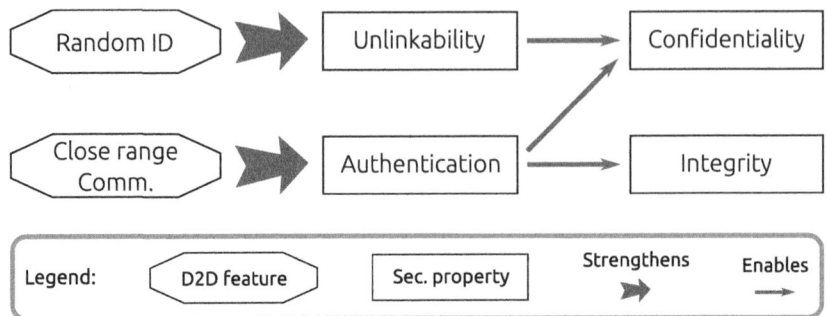

Fig. 5. Some of D2D communication's features strengthen our desired security properties.

Randomised Host Identifiers (Random ID). Internet communication stands atop the IP protocol of the third 'network' OSI layer. In the IP protocol, the IP address behaves like one's postal address on the net. It is a mandatory piece of metadata to provide while communicating: without it, your addressee cannot answer back to you. However, this piece of metadata jeopardises *unlinkability*, because it identifies a user, and can thus easily be used for tracking individuals online [59]. Hiding one's IP address remains possible through anonymity networks like Tor [29], but it is a cumbersome process, mostly undertaken by people in need for serious anonymity (e.g., journalists and whistleblowers).

On the other hand, we defined D2D communication as 'single hop' communication, taking no interest in routing messages through networks: D2D communication stands below, in the first ('physical') and second ('data link') network layers. Most often, data link is achieved through the MAC protocol. Similarly to IP, a layer-2 address is required to identify communicating hosts, notably in the advertising (broadcast) phase. Privacy-wise, this situation is bad, because such an address identifies a network card—thus its host device, and consequently its user. However, *there is no crucial need to broadcast one's* real *layer-2 address to establish and maintain a D2D connection.* Instead, this address can be randomly generated and periodically rotated by their host device to strengthen *unlinkability*. Efforts are indeed undertaken to hide this personal identifier by the most famous D2D channels:

- In the Wi-Fi realm, the effort of randomising the MAC address has initially been made by OS manufacturers, such as Linux Tails [76]. Although, IEEE 802.11 has been pushing MAC randomization since 2018 (as part of amendment 802.11aq), and created a task group entitled 'Randomized and Changing MAC Addresses' in 2021, specifically interested in anonymising MAC addresses without loss of utility for related services [41]. Indeed, several network operations traditionally depend on having fixed MAC addresses, such as MAC filtering or DHCP reservation;
- The Bluetooth 4.0 specification introduced the 'smart privacy' feature: it notably replaces one's broadcast MAC address with a random one, derived

from the real Bluetooth card MAC address [15]. The only way to retrieve the real MAC from the random one, is using the broadcaster's *Identity Resolution Key* (IRK). The IRK is only shared with remotes after pairing, meaning that only trusted peers are able to de-anonymise one's broadcast MAC address.

Having unlinkable communication sessions benefits *confidentiality*, because it hides real network identifiers from unauthorized parties. Furthermore, such randomized & evolving addresses preclude longitudinal location tracking, and thus also improve *context privacy*.

Close Range Communication. Digital authentication is the process of verifying one's identity, to ascertain that they are authorised to access specific pieces of information. Authentication revolves around the exchange and validation of cryptographic keys, that are then used to encrypt and sign future messages. To that regard, authentication enables both the *confidentiality* and *integrity* security properties.

Three factors are generally used to establish one's digital identity: **knowledge**, where the system verifies that the user *knows* a private information (password, PIN codes...); **possession**, where the system verifies that the user *owns* a physical object (computing device, token...); and lastly the **biometric factor**, where the system verifies something that the user *is* (fingerprints, face, eye scan...). Using Wi-Fi or Bluetooth, we are used to exchanging passwords, which constitute *knowledge factors*. Yet, authentication can be further facilitated by using physical proximity to assert a *possession factor*. *Close range communication* (e.g., NFC or QR code scanning) is a convincing way to ensure that a communication is initiated between two legitimate users, as both assert that they are the ones *owning* the communicating devices. Furthermore, close range communication can be viewed as a bootstrap side-channel to exchange encryption keys, which eschews the need for e.g. Diffie-Hellman key exchanges (prone to man-in-the-middle attacks), and establishes a second authentication factor: *knowledge*.

Note that authentication does not necessarily imply the disclosure of one's *full* identity. Through cryptography, and with the help of a source of trust (such as a certificate authority), it becomes possible to ensure that one is authorized to access a service, without disclosing any other information. The process is called *anonymous authentication* [30,54], but cannot be easily carried out without the help of a third-party (outside the D2D communication scope).

5.4 Authentication in Bluetooth and Wi-Fi

Since their inception, both channels allow for open or password-protected authentication of peers. While Wi-Fi networks hold long-term passwords, in some cases Bluetooth employs one-time PIN codes (which only need to be matched on both pairing devices). In Bluetooth, the initial authentication (pairing) is usually manual. Because devices exchange encryption keys (such as the aforementioned IRK) while pairing, connecting already paired devices is automatic and much simpler: the devices recognize and connect to each other, without the need for human intervention. In 2007, the Wi-Fi Alliance proposed *Wi-Fi Protected Setup* (WPS) to ease network onboarding, notably featuring a PIN code scheme similar to Bluetooth's. Sadly, WPS' PIN code mode contained a vulnerability, allowing an attacker to brute-force the PIN code under certain conditions [82].

Wi-Fi Easy Connect (WEC) [88] was introduced in 2018 to further ease network authentication of interface-less IoT devices. WEC connects such a device (called 'enrollee') to a wireless network by using a third-party 'configurator' (smartphone or else). By scanning a QR code or NFC tag on the enrollee, the configurator initiates a secure connection with it to exchange information about the Wi-Fi access point and the connecting device. Through the configurator, the enrollee then gets clearance, and can finally connect to the network by itself. This process constitutes an example of close range communication for authentication, as discussed above.

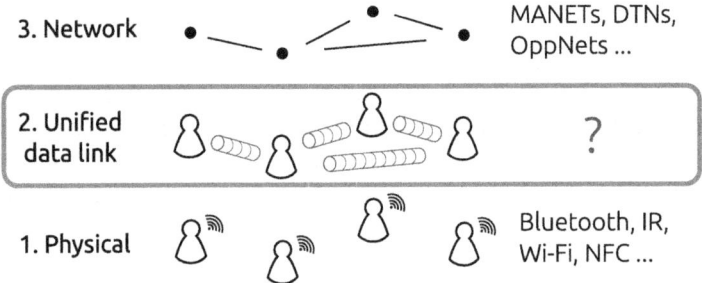

Fig. 6. The literature lacks a standard abstraction to unify D2D channels in the link layer.

6 Conclusion

This survey article took interest in the adoption state of D2D communication for end-users. We motivated the importance of this communication paradigm in terms of environmental sustainability, privacy and disparities in access to broadband Internet. An online poll showed that usage scenarios where D2D communication would be beneficial exist in the wild. The state of the practice in communication channels was then reviewed, as well as the paradigm's security models. The path seems clear: device-to-device is needed and timely, many solutions exist, with interesting security features. So why such a low adoption rate?

A major technical hurdle remains—D2D communication's underwhelming support in operating systems. All existing APIs are either channel-specific and low-level or proprietary, Apple has never allowed Bluetooth file transfer, Android's Wi-Fi ad-hoc APIs are impractical (e.g. randomized hotspot SSID and password), etc. The variety of Bluetooth's hardware & software implementations is often pointed at to explain its underwhelming performances on certain device pairs. Further study should be undertaken to quantify the extent of these alleged compatibility issues. As illustrated in Fig. 6, the authors believe that a higher-level cross-platform API encompassing several communication channels would ease development. Similarly to the IP stack, such an API would abstract the physical layer below more practical link-oriented controls. Indeed, all D2D channels follow the same communication process: discovery (beaconing & scanning), optionally followed by an authorization and a connected phase. Going a step further, a unified network layer would be beneficial for transparent multi-hop D2D routing. Two decades of research on infrastructure-less networks have scrutinized the topic, e.g. *Mobile Ad hoc Networks* (MANETs), *Delay-Tolerant Networks* (DTNs), and *Opportunistic Networks* (OppNets) [22,27,80]. We hope that this article motivates the adoption of more local communication processes, and provide a solid ground to continue advancing toward this end.

References

1. 3GPP: Release 12. Standard v0.2.0, 3GPP (2015)
2. 3GPP: Release 15. Standard v15.0.0, 3GPP (2019)
3. Aernouts, M., Berkvens, R., Van Vlaenderen, K., Weyn, M.: Sigfox and LoRaWAN datasets for fingerprint localization in large urban and rural areas. Data **3**(2), 13 (2018). https://doi.org/10.3390/data3020013
4. Al-Saggaf, Y.: The use of data mining by private health insurance companies and customers' privacy: an ethical analysis. Cambridge Q. Healthcare Ethics **24**(3), 281–292 (2015). https://doi.org/10.1017/S0963180114000607
5. Antonioli, D., Tippenhauer, N.O., Rasmussen, K.B.: Nearby threats: reversing, analyzing, and attacking Google's 'nearby connections' on android. In: Proceedings 2019 Network and Distributed System Security Symposium. Internet Society, San Diego, CA (2019). https://doi.org/10.14722/ndss.2019.23367
6. Apple: AirPlay (2022). https://www.apple.com/airplay/. Accessed Apr 2023
7. Apple: Nearby interactions with u1 (2022). https://developer.apple.com/nearby-interaction/. Accessed Apr 2023
8. Apple Fandom: iPhone (1st generation) (2023). https://apple.fandom.com/wiki/IPhone_(1st_generation). Accessed Apr 2023
9. Apple Support: Ultra Wideband Availability (2021). https://support.apple.com/en-us/HT212274. Accessed Apr 2023
10. Asghari, H., van Eeten, M., Bauer, J.M., Mueller, M.: Deep packet inspection: effects of regulation on its deployment by internet providers. SSRN Scholarly Paper ID 2242463, Social Science Research Network, Rochester, NY, September 2013. https://doi.org/10.2139/ssrn.2242463
11. Augustin, A., Yi, J., Clausen, T., Townsley, W.M.: A study of LoRa: long range & low power networks for the Internet of Things. Sensors (Basel, Switzerland) **16**(9), 1466 (2016). https://doi.org/10.3390/s16091466
12. Barrett, B.: The Biggest iPhone News Is a Tiny New Chip Inside It. Wired, December 2019)
13. Bays, B.A., Mc Gowan, M.J.: Use of RFID for tracking government property - proof of concept/pilot (2017). https://www.osti.gov/biblio/1456529. Accessed Apr 2023
14. Bluetooth SIG: Bluetooth Core Specification. Standard v 1.0B, Bluetooth SIG (1999)

15. Bluetooth SIG: Bluetooth Technology Protecting Your Privacy (2015). https://www.bluetooth.com/blog/bluetooth-technology-protecting-your-privacy/. Accessed May 2023
16. Bluetooth SIG: Bluetooth Core Specification. Standard v 5.0, Bluetooth SIG (2016)
17. Bluetooth SIG: Bluetooth Technology Overview (2023). https://www.bluetooth.com/learn-about-bluetooth/tech-overview/. Accessed Apr 2023
18. Bluetooth SIG: Bluetooth® Core Specification Version 5.4 - Technical Overview, February 2023. https://www.bluetooth.com/bluetooth-resources/bluetooth-core-specification-version-5-4-technical-overview/. Accessed Apr 2023
19. Bluetooth SIG: Understanding Bluetooth Range (2023). https://www.bluetooth.com/learn-about-bluetooth/key-attributes/range/. Accessed Apr 2023
20. Cable.co.uk: Worldwide mobile data pricing 2021 (2021). https://www.cable.co.uk/mobiles/worldwide-data-pricing/. Accessed Apr 2023
21. Cadwalladr, C.: 'I Made Steve Bannon's Psychological Warfare Tool': Meet the Data War Whistleblower. The Guardian, March 2018
22. Cc, S., Raychoudhury, V., Marfia, G., Singla, A.: A survey of routing and data dissemination in delay tolerant networks. J. Netw. Comput. App. **67**, 128–146 (2016). https://doi.org/10.1016/j.jnca.2016.01.002
23. Cheng, J.: Over 3 Years Later, "Deleted" Facebook Photos Are Still Online. Ars Technica, February 2012
24. Cisco: Annual Interet Report (2018-2023) White Paper. Technical report, Cisco (2020)
25. Conti, M., Passarella, A., Das, S.K.: The Internet of People (IoP): a new wave in pervasive mobile computing. Pervas. Mobile Comput. **41**, 1–27 (2017). https://www.sciencedirect.com/science/article/pii/S1574119217303723
26. Cook, D.J., Das, S.K.: Pervasive computing at scale: transforming the state of the art. Pervas. Mobile Comput. **8**(1), 22–35 (2012). https://www.sciencedirect.com/science/article/pii/S1574119211001416
27. Corson, S., Macker, J.: Mobile Ad hoc Networking (MANET): Routing Protocol Performance Issues and Evaluation Considerations. Technical report. RFC2501, RFC Editor, January 1999. https://doi.org/10.17487/rfc2501
28. Court of Justice of the European Union: Judgment on traffic log retention in the face of national security. Court judgment ECLI:EU:C:2020:791, October 2020
29. Dingledine, R., Mathewson, N., Syverson, P.: Tor: The Second-Generation Onion Router. Technical report, Defense Technical Information Center, Fort Belvoir, VA, January 2004. https://doi.org/10.21236/ADA465464
30. Feng, W., Yan, Z., Yang, L.T., Zheng, Q.: Anonymous authentication on trust in blockchain-based mobile crowdsourcing. IEEE Internet Things J. (2020). https://doi.org/10.1109/JIOT.2020.3018878
31. Google: Nearby Connections API (2022). https://developers.google.com/nearby/connections/. Accessed Apr 2023
32. Google: Wi-Fi Aware overview | Android Documentation (2023). https://developer.android.com/guide/topics/connectivity/wifi-aware. Accessed Apr 2023
33. GSMA: Over half world's population now using mobile internet (2021). https://www.gsma.com/newsroom/press-release/over-half-worlds-population-now-using-mobile-internet/. Accessed Apr 2023
34. Haus, M., Waqas, M., Ding, A.Y., Li, Y., Tarkoma, S., Ott, J.: Security and privacy in device-to-device (D2D) communication: a review. IEEE Commun. Surv. Tutor. **19**(2), 1054–1079 (2017). https://doi.org/10.1109/COMST.2017.2649687

35. IEEE: IEEE Standard for Wireless LAN Medium Access Control (MAC) and Physical Layer (PHY) specifications. Standard, IEEE Std 802.11-1997, November 1997. https://doi.org/10.1109/IEEESTD.1997.85951
36. IEEE: IEEE Standard for Telecommunications and Information Exchange Between Systems - LAN/MAN Specific Requirements - Part 11: Wireless Medium Access Control (MAC) and physical layer (PHY) specifications: High Speed Physical Layer in the 5 GHz band. Standard, IEEE Std 802.11a-1999, December 1999. https://doi.org/10.1109/IEEESTD.1999.90606
37. IEEE: IEEE Standard for Information Technology - Telecommunications and information exchange between systems - Local and Metropolitan networks - Specific requirements - Part 11: Wireless LAN Medium Access Control (MAC) and Physical Layer (PHY) specifications: Higher Speed Physical Layer (PHY) Extension in the 2.4 GHz band. Standard, IEEE Std 802.11b-1999, January 2000. https://doi.org/10.1109/IEEESTD.2000.90914
38. IEEE: IEEE Standard for Low-Rate Wireless Networks. Standard, IEEE Std 802.15.4-2020 (Revision of IEEE Std 802.15.4-2015), July 2020. https://doi.org/10.1109/IEEESTD.2020.9144691
39. IEEE: IEEE Standard for Information Technology–Telecommunications and Information Exchange between Systems Local and Metropolitan Area Networks–Specific Requirements Part 11: Wireless LAN Medium Access Control (MAC) and Physical Layer (PHY) Specifications Amendment 1: Enhancements for High-Efficiency WLAN. Standard, IEEE Std 802.11ax-2021 (Amendment to IEEE Std 802.11-2020), May 2021. https://doi.org/10.1109/IEEESTD.2021.9442429
40. IEEE: IEEE Standard for Information Technology–Telecommunications and Information Exchange between Systems Local and Metropolitan Area Networks–Specific Requirements Part 11: Wireless LAN Medium Access Control (MAC) and Physical Layer (PHY) Specifications Amendment 2: Enhanced Throughput for Operation in License-exempt Bands above 45 GHz. Standard, IEEE Std 802.11ay-2021 (Amendment to IEEE Std 802.11-2020 as amendment by IEEE Std 802.11ax-2021), July 2021. https://doi.org/10.1109/IEEESTD.2021.9502046
41. IEEE: IEEE P802.11 - TASK GROUP BH (RCM). Meeting update (2022). https://ieee802.org/11/Reports/tgbh_update.htm. Accessed May 2023
42. Infrared Data Association: Serial Infrared Physical Layer Specification. Standard v1.4 (2001)
43. International Energy Agency (IEA): The Role of Critical Minerals in Clean Energy Transitions. Technical report, May 2021
44. Internet world stats: Internet usage statistics (2021). https://internetworldstats.com/stats.htm, Accessed Apr 2023
45. Islim, M.S., Haas, H.: Modulation techniques for Li-Fi. ZTE Commun. **14** (2016)
46. ISO Standards: ISO/IEC 18092:2004 — Information technology — Telecommunications and information exchange between systems — Near Field Communication — Interface and Protocol. Standard (2004)
47. ISO Standards: ISO/IEC 26907:2007 — Information technology — Automatic Telecommunications and information exchange between systems — High Rate Ultra Wideband PHY and MAC Standard. Standard (2007)
48. ISO Standards: ISO/IEC 26908:2007 — Information technology — Automatic Telecommunications and information exchange between systems — MAC-PHY Interface for ISO/IEC 26907. Standard (2007)
49. ISO Standards: ISO/IEC 18004:2015 — Information technology — Automatic identification and data capture techniques — QR Code bar code symbology specification. Standard, February 2015

50. Jameel, F., Hamid, Z., Jabeen, F., Zeadally, S., Javed, M.A.: A survey of device-to-device communications: research issues and challenges. IEEE Commun. Surv. Tutor. **20**(3), 2133–2168 (2018). https://doi.org/10.1109/COMST.2018.2828120
51. Kar, U.N., Sanyal, D.K.: A critical review of 3GPP standardization of device-to-device communication in cellular networks. SN Comput. Sci. **1**(1), 1–18 (2019). https://doi.org/10.1007/s42979-019-0045-5
52. Lavric, A., Petrariu, A.I., Popa, V.: SigFox Communication Protocol: The New Era of IoT? In: 2019 International Conference on Sensing and Instrumentation in IoT Era (ISSI), pp. 1–4, August 2019. https://doi.org/10.1109/ISSI47111.2019.9043727
53. Li, A.: Pixel 6 Pro UWB, adjust Assistant long press, Pixel Buds A-Series bass slider, & more, December 2021. https://9to5google.com/2021/12/06/december-pixel-feature-drop-android-12/. Accessed Apr 2023
54. Lindell, Y.: Anonymous authentication. J. Priv. Confid. **2**(2), 1-10 (2011). https://doi.org/10.29012/jpc.v2i2.590
55. Luxey, A.: E-Squads: A Novel Paradigm to Build Privacy-Preserving Ubiquitous Applications. Ph.D. thesis, Université de Rennes, November 2019
56. Matz, S.C., Kosinski, M., Nave, G., Stillwell, D.J.: Psychological targeting as an effective approach to digital mass persuasion. Proc. Natl. Acad. Sci. **114**(48), 12714–12719 (2017). https://doi.org/10.1073/pnas.1710966114
57. Mcclain, C.: 34% of Lower-Income Home Broadband Users Have Had Trouble Paying for Their Service amid COVID-19. Pew Research Center, June 2021
58. Mekki, K., Bajic, E., Chaxel, F., Meyer, F.: Overview of cellular LPWAN technologies for IoT deployment: Sigfox, LoRaWAN, and NB-IoT. In: 2018 IEEE International Conference on Pervasive Computing and Communications Workshops (PerCom Workshops), pp. 197–202, March 2018. https://doi.org/10.1109/PERCOMW.2018.8480255
59. Mishra, V., Laperdrix, P., Vastel, A., Rudametkin, W., Rouvoy, R., Lopatka, M.: Don't count me out: on the relevance of IP address in the tracking ecosystem. In: Proceedings of The Web Conference 2020. WWW 2020, ACM, New York, NY, USA (2020). https://doi.org/10.1145/3366423.3380161
60. Nakashima, E., Warrick, J.: For NSA Chief, Terrorist Threat Drives Passion to 'Collect It All'. Washington Post, July 2013
61. Campbell, N.: QR Code Contact Tracing. Vaccine Passports Becoming New Normal in Europe. America, Vision Times, January 2021
62. Nieva, R.: Google's Pixel 6 phones are coming with a chip designed in-house, August 2021. https://www.cnet.com/tech/mobile/googles-pixel-6-phones-are-coming-with-a-chip-the-apple-rival-designed-in-house/. Accessed Apr 2023
63. Nintendo Wiki: List of Nintendo systems (2022). https://nintendo.fandom.com/wiki/List_of_Nintendo_systems. Accessed Apr 2023
64. Pirch, H.J., Leong, F.: Introduction to Impulse Radio UWB Seamless Access Systems. White paper, FiRa Consortium (2020)
65. Price, R.: Google Drive now hosts more than 2 trillion files. Business Insider, May 2017
66. Primault, V., Boutet, A., Mokhtar, S.B., Brunie, L.: The long road to computational location privacy: a survey. IEEE Commun. Surv. Tutor. **21**(3), 2772–2793 (2019). https://doi.org/10.1109/COMST.2018.2873950
67. Rowan-Robinson, M.: Night Vision: Exploring the Infrared Universe. Cambridge University Press, Cambridge (2012)

68. Sairam, K., Gunasekaran, N., Redd, S.: Bluetooth in wireless communication. IEEE Commun. Mag. **40**(6), 90–96 (2002). https://doi.org/10.1109/MCOM.2002.1007414
69. Secure Mobile Networking Lab: OpenDrop: An Open Source AirDrop Implementation, August 2022. https://github.com/seemoo-lab/opendrop. Accessed Apr 2023
70. Shen, W., Hong, W., Cao, X., Yin, B., Shila, D.M., Cheng, Y.: Secure key establishment for device-to-device communications. In: 2014 IEEE Global Communications Conference, pp. 336–340, December 2014. https://doi.org/10.1109/GLOCOM.2014.7036830
71. Shiu, Y.S., Chang, S., Wu, H.C., Huang, S., Chen, H.H.: Physical layer security in wireless networks: a tutorial. IEEE Wirel. Commun. **18**(2), 66–74 (2011). https://doi.org/10.1109/MWC.2011.5751298
72. Cooper, S.: Ultra Wideband & You. WLPC Phoenix, March 2020. https://www.youtube.com/watch?v=TR-rahy3Y2k. Accessed Apr 2023
73. Stute, M., Kreitschmann, D., Hollick, M.: One billion apples' secret sauce: recipe for the apple wireless direct link ad hoc protocol. In: Proceedings of the 24th Annual International Conference on Mobile Computing and Networking, pp. 529–543, October 2018. https://doi.org/10.1145/3241539.3241566
74. Stute, M., Kreitschmann, D., Hollick, M.: The Open Wireless Link Project (2018). https://owlink.org
75. Stute, M., et al.: A billion open interfaces for eve and Mallory: MitM, DoS, and tracking attacks on iOS and macOS through apple wireless direct link. In: 28th USENIX Security Symposium (USENIX Security 2019), pp. 37–54 (2019)
76. Tails: MAC address anonymization. Documentation (2022). https://tails.boum.org/contribute/design/MAC_address/. Accessed May 2023
77. Toh, C.K., Chen, R., Delwar, M., Allen, D.: Experimenting with an Ad Hoc wireless network on campus: insights and experiences. ACM SIGMETRICS Perform. Eval. Rev. **28**(3), 21–29 (2000). https://doi.org/10.1145/377616.377622
78. Toh, C.K., Delwar, M., Allen, D.: Evaluating the communication performance of an Ad Hoc wireless network. IEEE Trans. Wirel. Commun. **1**(3), 402–414 (2002). https://doi.org/10.1109/TWC.2002.800539
79. Toh, C.K.: Routing Method for Ad-Hoc Mobile Networks, November 1999
80. Trifunovic, S., Kouyoumdjieva, S.T., Distl, B., Pajevic, L., Karlsson, G., Plattner, B.: A decade of research in opportunistic networks: challenges, relevance, and future directions. IEEE Commun. Mag. **55**(1), 168–173 (2017). https://doi.org/10.1109/MCOM.2017.1500527CM
81. United Nations: With almost half of world's population still offline, digital divide risks becoming 'new face of inequality', deputy secretary-general warns general assembly (2021). https://www.un.org/press/en/2021/dsgsm1579.doc.htm. Accessed Apr 2023
82. Viehböck, S.: Brute forcing Wi-Fi Protected Setup, December 2011. https://www.cs.cmu.edu/~rdriley/330/papers/viehboeck_wps.pdf. Accessed May 2023
83. Vogels, E.A.: Some digital divides persist between rural, urban and suburban America. Pew Res. Center **19** (2021)
84. Wang, M., Yan, Z.: A survey on security in D2D communications. Mobile Netw. App. **22**(2), 195–208 (2016). https://doi.org/10.1007/s11036-016-0741-5
85. Want, R.: An introduction to RFID technology. IEEE Pervas. Comput. **5**, 25–33 (2006). https://doi.org/10.1109/MPRV.2006.2
86. Weis, S.A.: RFID. Radio Frequency IDentification, Principles and Applications (2007)

87. Wi-Fi Alliance: Discover Wi-Fi Direct (2023). https://www.wi-fi.org/discover-wi-fi/wi-fi-direct. Accessed Apr 2023
88. Wi-Fi Alliance: Discover Wi-Fi Easy Connect (2023). https://www.wi-fi.org/discover-wi-fi/wi-fi-easy-connect. Accessed Apr 2023
89. Wi-Fi Alliance: Wi-Fi Aware (2023). https://www.wi-fi.org/discover-wi-fi/wi-fi-aware. Accessed Apr 2023
90. Wikipedia: List of Bluetooth profiles (2022). https://en.wikipedia.org/wiki/List_of_Bluetooth_profiles. Accessed Apr 2023
91. Wikipedia: Internet traffic (2023). https://en.wikipedia.org/wiki/Internet_traffic. Accessed May 2023
92. Xiaomi Inc.: Mi Remote controller - for TV, STB, AC and more – Apps on Google Play (2022). https://play.google.com/store/apps/details?id=com.duokan.phone.remotecontroller. Accessed Apr 2023
93. Zuboff, S.: The Age of Surveillance Capitalism: The Fight for a Human Future at the New Frontier of Power. PublicAffairs, New York (2019)

Multi-provider Capabilities in EnOSlib: Driving Distributed System Experiments on the Edge-to-Cloud Continuum

Baptiste Jonglez[1]✉, Matthieu Simonin[2], Jolan Philippe[2], and Sidi Mohammed Kaddour[1]

[1] Nantes Université, Ecole Centrale Nantes, IMT Atlantique, CNRS, Inria, LS2N, UMR 6004, 44000 Nantes, France
{baptiste.jonglez,sidi-mohammed.kaddour}@inria.fr
[2] University of Rennes, Inria, CNRS, IRISA, UMR 6074, Rennes, France
{matthieu.simonin,jolan.philippe}@inria.fr

Abstract. This paper introduces recent advances in EnOSlib, a Python library that aims at facilitating the design and execution of reproducible experiments across distributed computing infrastructures. Originally developed to simplify experimentation on testbeds such as Grid'5000 and Chameleon Cloud, EnOSlib now incorporates support multi-provider deployments, including access to edge resources, as well as advanced services.

Key contributions include integration with Kwollect for fine-grained energy measurements, a planning service for executing timed events, and enhanced network emulation functionalities. These features enable users to model and study complex, realistic scenarios such as latency-sensitive edge-to-cloud applications.

A major new capability is the support for synchronized multi-infrastructure experiments, allowing simultaneous resource reservation and deployment across diverse testbeds. The paper illustrates these capabilities through a distributed video processing use case spanning edge and cloud platforms.

This paper is the companion paper of the tutorial presented in DAIS 2025.

Keywords: Experiment-driven research · Performance evaluation · Multiple infrastructure · Distributed computing experimentation library

1 Introduction

This paper is the companion paper of a tutorial presented in DAIS 2025. The tutorial showcases the EnOSlib [8] library: a largely adopted Python library[1]

---
[1] https://discovery.gitlabpages.inria.fr/enoslib/theyuseit.html.

to ease distributed experimentation on different testbeds [7,9,12,16–18,20,21], and which is now also adopted by other frameworks [22,23]. We highlight how experiments for an edge-to-cloud use case can be expressed and run with EnOSlib.

EnOSlib targets established research testbeds such as Grid'5000 [6], FIT IoT-LAB [3] and Chameleon Cloud [15], and is also planning to interface with new testbeds like SLICES [2] or FABRIC [5]. The experimenter can leverage EnOSlib to obtain *resources* on these testbeds, such as bare-metal servers, virtual machines, IoT devices, isolated networks... It is then possible to develop and automate complete distributed experiments using these resources. As illustrated in Fig. 1, the key steps EnOSlib aims at dealing with are: (i) provisioning resources on which to run experiments, (ii) the management of these resources (e.g. configuration management, software setup), (iii) benchmarking and obtaining metrics from the experiments, and (iv) cleaning and/or destroying used resources.

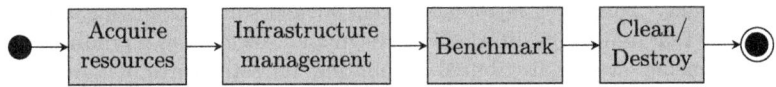

Fig. 1. General experimental workflow with EnOSlib.

Beyond the initial deployment of an application, EnOSlib facilitates the study of distributed systems by providing out-of-the box observability tools (e.g. off-the-shelves monitoring stacks) and variability injection functionalities (e.g. using state-of-art network emulation features). In the following we remind the core abstractions behind EnOSlib: *Provider* and *Service*, as well as an important design choice: *idempotency*.

Provider. At the EnOSlib's core lies the `Provider` abstraction. Providers connect to the various infrastructure to claim resources from. EnOSlib supports two types of resources: compute servers and networks (IPv4 or IPv6). In other words, a provider can be seen as a function that transforms an abstract resource description into a concrete set of `Hosts` and `Networks` with the side effect of actually claiming the corresponding resource on the platforms. An example of user script is given in Fig. 2. The `Host` and `Network` object are generic in the sense that a user can interact the same way with those objects regardless of their provenance. This allows *decoupling* between hardware resources specification (different for each platform and each situation to evaluate) and the actual actions to perform during the experiments (common and generic). In practice, that means that an experimentation can be transferred to another testbed at the cost of changing only the provider used, assuming that the experiment doesn't rely on testbed-specific services.

EnOSlib is shipped with providers for Grid'5000 (bare-metal and virtual machines), Chameleon (bare-metal, cloud and edge containers), IoT-LAB (embedded IoT devices), Vagrant (virtual machines on the local machine). The provider abstraction has been extended to optionally let the users get resources on different testbeds *at the same time*: this new feature is presented in Sect. 2.3.

```
1  provider_conf = {
2    "job_name": "myjobname",
3    "resources": {
4      "machines": [{
5        "roles": ["server"],
6        "cluster": "paradoxe",
7        "nodes": 1,
8      }, {
9        "roles": ["client"],
10       "cluster": "paradoxe",
11       "nodes": 3,
12     }
13   ],
14  }
15 }
16 provider = (
17   en.G5k.from_dictionary(conf)
18 )
19 roles, nets = provider.init()
```

```
1  provider_conf = {
2    "lease_name": "mylease",
3    "resources": {
4      "machines": [{
5        "roles": ["server"],
6        "flavour": "compute_skylake",
7        "number": 1,
8      }, {
9        "roles": ["client"],
10       "flavour": "compute_skylake",
11       "number": 3,
12     }
13   ],
14  }
15 }
16 conf = (
17   en.CBMConf
18     .from_dictionary(provider_conf)
19 )
20 provider = en.CBM(conf)
21 roles, nets = provider.init()
```

Fig. 2. Resources specification and grouping resources into *generic roles* on Grid'5000 (left) and Chameleon (right). The `roles` returned by the provider can be queried to get a group of hosts. For instance `roles["client"]` returns a set of 3 `Hosts` corresponding to 3 (concrete) servers labelled as `client` by the user.

Services. A `Service` is a high-level construction that relies on the resource abstraction to provide reusable "units of behavior". It is instantiated through a Python function call that enforces its configuration as a side effect. Concretely, a `Service` bootstraps classical software stacks on the resources and hides the low-level details of their deployment to the experimenter (although experimenters have to feed the service with specific inputs described in its interface). EnOSlib offers a growing set of `Services` based on user needs. It includes several *Observability* `Services` that can deploy various monitoring/tracing stacks depending on the user needs. *Network emulation* `Services` can be used to get control over bandwidth and latency of network interface. *Software stacks* `Services` are able to deploy complex software stack (e.g. Kubernetes). A recently added `Service` is described in Sect. 2.2.

Idempotency. Idempotency refers to the property of an operation: applying it multiple times must give the same output as applying it a single time. This property has been popularized by Ansible in the context of configuration management systems. Idempotency is a key property to support repeatability and robustness in experimental workflows. It also facilitates iterative experiment development using Jupyter Notebooks, since a given block of code can be re-executed as many times as necessary. EnOSlib ensures a first level of idempotency internally, and also relies on Ansible modules to help the experimenter write idempotent code. An example of user script to perform actions is given in Listing 1.1.

Listing 1.1. Actions on resource described in Fig. 2 using the *generic roles*. Since roles are defined for both resources on Grid'5000 and Chameleon Cloud, triggering actions on distant machines is expressed in the same way. In this example, the server generates a configuration file before copying it on each client. Then, the clients use the copied file as input for a local program. Behind the scenes, the `play_on` invocation generates an Ansible playbook, giving access to all standard Ansible modules (`shell`, `copy`...), encouraging experimenters to write idempotent code.

```
1  # On the server: generate a configuration file
2  with play_on(pattern_hosts="server") as p:
3      p.shell("echo 'parameter=value' > /tmp/my_config.conf")
4
5  # Copy the config file to all clients
6  server_host = roles["server"][0].address # get the server IP
7  with play_on(pattern_hosts="client") as p:
8      # Fetch the config file from the server
9      p.copy(
10         src=f"{server_host}:/tmp/my_config.conf",
11         dest="/tmp/my_config.conf",
12         remote_src=True
13     )
14
15 # On each client: run a command using the config file
16 with play_on(pattern_hosts="client") as p:
17     p.command("./my_program --config /tmp/my_config.conf")
```

The paper is organized as follows. First, Sect. 2 introduces the new features added in EnOSlib since the reference publication [8]. In Sect. 3, the use case for the tutorial is presented, and the methodology to experiment on it is presented in Sect. 4. Sections 5 and 6 respectively present how to deploy the experiment on a multi-site and on a multi-provider context. Concluding remarks are given in Sect. 7.

2 New EnOSlib Features

Building upon the concepts introduced in earlier work on EnOSlib [8], this section presents recent advancements that expand the library features. Notable additions include (i) a support for *metrics collection* with Kwollect [10]

(Sect. 2.1); (ii) a *planning service* for mocking events allowing their reproducibility (Sect. 2.2), and (iii) *multi-provider* functionalities enabling seamless experiments across heterogeneous testbeds (Sect. 2.3). Beyond the core library, EnOSlib can also take advantage of Jupyter notebooks to interactively design, execute, and visualize results, including infrastructure introspection and live data previews (Sect. 2.4).

2.1 Metrics Collection with the Kwollect Service

Energy efficiency is becoming more and more critical when evaluating algorithms and distributed systems. While software-based energy measurement tools such as PowerAPI [11], Kepler [4], Scaphandre [1], or PowerJoular [19] have been growing in popularity, they rely on specific vendor functionalities (e.g. Intel RAPL) or estimation models (e.g. regression models based on CPU usage). As a result, they have limited precision and frequency, and they cannot measure the energy impact of some components such as the physical disks or the Power Supplies Units (PSU).

Fine-grained energy measurements at the physical level allow to fully evaluate and compare the energy efficiency of different algorithms on a given piece of hardware; alternatively, the energy consumption of a single algorithm can be measured on different hardware (for example with and without GPU). Most interestingly, high-frequency energy measurements open interesting use-cases such as measuring the energy impact of memory transfers or disk I/O operations.

EnOSlib supports experiments requiring accurate and fine-grained energy measurement through integration with Kwollect [10], a monitoring solution available on the Grid'5000 platform [6]. Kwollect continuously polls physical wattmetres at high frequency and exposes collected data through an API. It also collects power consumption metrics from other physical sources such as Power Distribution Units (PDUs), or the network traffic from network equipment. Beyond Kwollect, other energy monitoring systems could be integrated in EnOSlib as long as they provide an API that EnOSlib can query.

In practice, the experimenter specifies which sections of the experiment should be monitored for energy consumption, and then EnOSlib retrieves energy traces from the Kwollect API using the correct time ranges.

In keeping with the general philosophy of EnOSlib as a library, the rest of the experiment is the responsibility of the experimenter: running the actual workload, and performing data analysis on the energy measurement data. Example code is shown in Listing 1.2 with resulting data shown in Fig. 3.

2.2 Events Planning

Distributed deployments in the wild are subject to various events like the loss of connectivity between communicating processes, nodes failures, additions/removal of resource capabilities, transient resource limitations, ... Distributed systems experiments is also about studying the behaviour of systems in the face

Listing 1.2. Example EnOSlib code that collects power measurement from Kwollect during a CPU stress test. The result is shown in Figure 3

```
# Allocate resources (here, physical servers on G5K)
conf = en.G5kConf() \
    .add_machine(roles=["server"], cluster="nova", nodes=1)
    .add_machine(roles=["server"], cluster="taurus", nodes=1)

# Setup monitoring API
monitor = en.Kwollect(nodes=roles["server"])
monitor.deploy()

# Run a loop of stress tests under the monitor
monitor.start()
duration = 2
time.sleep(duration)
for cpu_cores in [1, 2, 8, 14, 20, 26, 32]:
    en.run_command(f"stress-ng --cpu {cpu_cores} -t {duration}",
                   roles=roles["server"])
time.sleep(duration)
monitor.stop()

# Fetch monitoring data from Kwollect API between start and stop
data = monitor.get_metrics(metrics=["wattmetre_power_watt"])
```

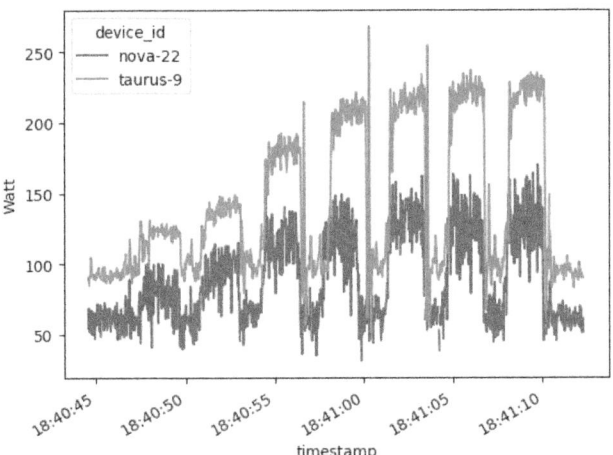

Fig. 3. Power consumption result obtained with EnOSlib using physical wattmetres (two different physical servers during a CPU stress test)

of such events. EnOSlib exposes a Planning service allowing the experimenter to schedule events at a specific time. This serves two purposes (1) *expressivity*:

a user can easily describe a sequence of events and (2) *reproducibility*: the same scenario can be replayed. In EnOSlib an event is an action to run at a specific date on a specific set of hosts. Different types of events are currently supported and showcased in Fig. 4: `StartEvent` that are used to start a process given a command line, `KillEvent` that is used to terminate a set of processes (e.g. to simulate process crashes) and a `CGroupEvent` used to schedule cgroup changes (e.g. to throttle some resources: CPU, IOs ...). The `Planning` service of EnOSlib is a collection of events and is responsible to run the various actions in a timely manner on a distributed set of Hosts. This service is inspired by MockFog [13] which used such approach to evaluate edge use cases: the EnOSlib `Planning` service makes the approach re-usable for other experiments.

```
1   ps = en.PlanningService()
2
3   ps.add_event(
4     en.StartEvent(
5       date=t1
6       cmd="stress -c 30",
7       host=roles["groupA"],
8       name=f"mysleep"
9     )
10  )
11
12  ps.add_event(
13    en.CGroupEvent(
14      date=t2
15      cpath="cpuset.cpus",
16      value="1-10",
17      host=roles["groupA"],
18      name=f"mysleep"
19    )
20  )
21  ps.add_event(
22    en.CGroupEvent(
23      date=t3
24      cpath="cpuset.cpus",
25      value="0-31",
26      host=roles["groupA"],
27      name=f"mysleep"
28    )
29  )
30
31  # Deploy the planning while
32  # monitoring the usage using dstat
33  with en.Dstat(nodes=roles["groupA"]):
34    ps.deploy()
35    # waiting a bit
36    time.sleep(
37      ps.until_end.total_seconds() + 60
38    )
```

Fig. 4. Pseudo code showing the use of the planning service. Line 1 to 29, the planning service is fed with some events: a stress process will be started at `t1`, the available cores to this process identified by its name will be then reduced from time `t2` to `t3`. Finally the user can draw the CPU usage during the execution of the planning thanks to the Dstat monitoring service that tracks some basic system metrics.

2.3 Experiment over Multiple Infrastructures

Experiments in the Fog/Edge context require heterogeneous resources (e.g. mixing IOT devices and large computing servers) and scalability (e.g. getting lot of the same resources). *Diversity* and *scalability* makes thus some experiments hard to perform on a single testbed. The provider abstraction offered by EnOSlib can be a solution since a single user script can embed calls to different providers. However this approach falls short when it comes to get the resources over different testbeds *at the same time*. Indeed depending on the platform status, resources might not be available or delayed. EnOSlib offers an elegant way to get resources over different platforms in a synchronized way: the *multi-provider* abstraction. The *multi-provider* abstraction is a new provider that ensures the resources over different platforms are acquired and released at the same time. This releases the user from the burden of writing the synchronization code by focusing on the experimentation logic. A user script is depicted in Fig. 5.

The synchronization algorithm consists in (1) querying each provider for a given time slot; if all providers agree on the time slot, then (2a) the slots are actually reserved; otherwise (2b) another time slot is tested. Testing a timeslot is provider-specific (some infrastructure expose the past and future resource status which can be leveraged to know in advance if a candidate time slot is actually possible). There is an obvious race condition between the step (1) and (2a) or (2b) since the state of the platform might have changed between the two phases. In the general case it is not a real problem especially when dealing with reservation far enough in the future.

```
1  # Naive multi-provider code.
2  # This is not robust.
3  import enoslib as en
4
5  g5k = en.G5k(conf_g5k)
6  roles_g5k, nets_g5k = g5k.init()
7
8  iot = en.Iotlab(iot_conf)
9  roles_iot, nets_iot = iot.init()
10
11 vms = en.Vagrant(vm_conf)
12 roles_vms, nets_vms = vms.init()
```

```
1  # Built-in multi-providers support.
2  # It ensures synchronized reservations.
3  import enoslib as en
4
5  g5k = en.G5k(conf_g5k)
6  iot = en.Iotlab(iot_conf)
7  vagrant = en.Vagrant(vagrant_conf)
8
9  roles, networks = en.Providers([
10     g5k,
11     iot_lab,
12     vagrant
13 ])
```

Fig. 5. Pseudo-codes illustrating the multi-provider use case. On the left the user uses three independent providers to get her resources on Grid'5000, IoT-LAB and local machine (Vagrant virtual machines). However resources may not be available or delayed on Grid'5000 or IoT-LAB due to the current platform availability. On the right the EnOSlib `Providers` instance can deal with different platforms, get resources in a synchronized way and return them as a regular `Provider`

2.4 Jupyter Integration

EnOSlib integrates with Jupyter notebooks, enabling users to interactively design, execute, and monitor infrastructure and experiments. This integration facilitates real-time introspection, live data visualization, and step-by-step experiment control, enhancing user experience.

To effectively display complex outputs within Jupyter notebooks, such as tables or plots, appropriate formatting is necessary. This may involve using specific display functions or formatting outputs as HTML or Markdown to ensure correct rendering. Notebook examples demonstrating these capabilities is available online.[2]

3 Edge-To-Cloud Use-Case: Distributed Video Processing

We will consider a common use-case throughout the tutorial: an edge-to-cloud video processing application designed to detect roaming animals[3]. Its high-level architecture is depicted in Fig. 6.

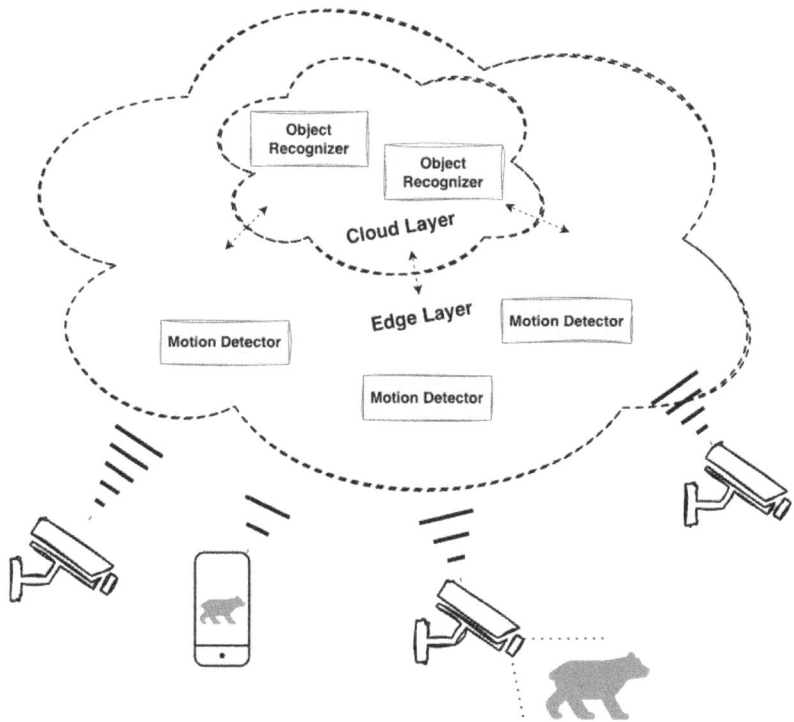

Fig. 6. Edge-to-cloud video processing application

This use-case is made of two main software components:

1. **Motion Detector**: Receives a video feed and continuously tries to detect motion in the images. Whenever a motion event is detected, the corresponding video frames are sent to the Object Recognizer for further analysis. This service typically runs on many small devices that are close to each video source to minimize the amount of data transfers.

---

[2] https://discovery.gitlabpages.inria.fr/enoslib/jupyter/.
[3] https://gitlab.inria.fr/STACK-RESEARCH-GROUP/software/edge-to-cloud-video-processing.

2. **Object Recognizer**: Receives video frames with motion events and tries to detect which object or animal is visible in the picture. This service typically has a single instance running in a cloud infrastructure.

The use-case includes a benchmark that consists of injecting a pre-recorded video feed with known parameters (configurable amount of motion over time, with a choice of several animals). It also includes advanced monitoring metrics from both the system and from the application itself (response time, frames per second...)

To deploy this use-case, we will use a simple topology with two Motion Detectors running on small servers such as Nvidia Jetson devices, and one Object Recognizer running on a regular server. This abstract deployment topology is show in Fig. 7. We will instantiate different variants of this deployment model during the tutorial.

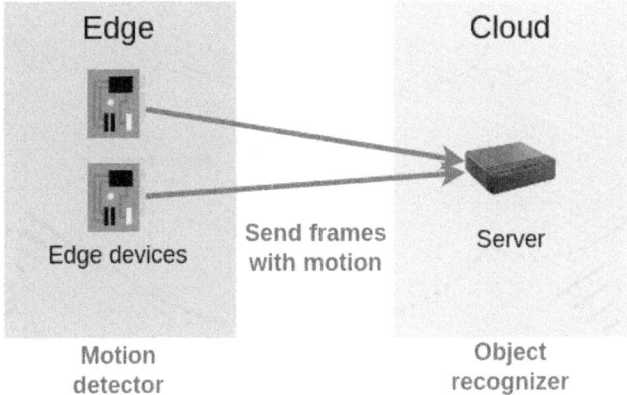

Fig. 7. The abstract deployment model we will use during the tutorial.

4 Methodology: From Network Emulation to Multi-provider Experiments

EnOSlib is well suited for experimenting with distributed system software: distributed databases, P2P systems, edge clusters... For this kind of experiments, we usually want to run the actual software (which rules out simulation) and we want to run it on real or virtualized hardware to obtain realistic system performance. However, we also want a high degree of control on the network, to be able to answer research questions such as: *What is the performance of my system under high network latency?*, or: *How does my distributed system behave when nodes get disconnected?*

In this situation, **network emulation** is a helpful tool: it allows to artificially introduce network issues, such as additional delay or packet loss, while running the real target software on a real testbed.

4.1 Step-By-Step Workflow

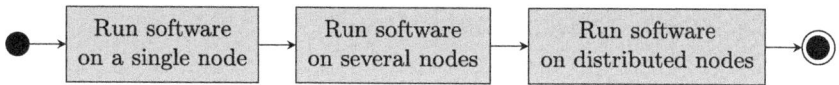

Fig. 8. Workflow for designing a complex distributed system experiment

When designing a complex distributed system experiment, a common workflow is the following:

1. run the target software on a single node to make sure that the deployment process works well (e.g. a virtual machine on the user laptop)
2. run the target software on several nodes connected by a local network, and use network emulation to study the target software under controlled conditions (e.g. run experiments with increasing latency and measure the resulting performance)
3. run the target software on distributed nodes, possibly on simultaneously on multiple platforms (e.g. Grid'5000, Chameleon Cloud, local infrastructure...), to study the target software under real network conditions

For each step of the workflow, the difficulty, cost and complexity of the deployment is increasing. To make sure that later steps work properly, the experimenter can rely on work done in previous steps to make the deployment more robust, building the experimental code in an iterative way.

4.2 Iterating Experiments

In experimental research, particularly when assessing system behavior under varying conditions, it is essential to ensure that each test iteration starts from a clean and consistent state. To ease systematic experimentation, it is beneficial to encapsulate the experimental workflow as illustrated in Fig. 8 – including resource reservation, setup, benchmark, resource teardown – within an atomic process (e.g. within a dedicated function).

This design ensures that each experiment is executed independently and that previous runs do not influence subsequent ones.

Listing 1.3 illustrates how to iterate over different network latencies using EnOSlib. For each latency value, the experiment reserves resources, sets up the environment (`setup_phase`), applies the specified network latency using Netem[4], runs the benchmark (`benchmark_phase`), and finally cleans up the resources using `destroy` functions.

---

[4] https://discovery.gitlabpages.inria.fr/enoslib/tutorials/network_emulation.html.

Listing 1.3. Typical pattern to iterate experiments with network emulation

```
1   import enoslib as en
2
3   LATENCIES = ["10ms", "20ms", "40ms", "100ms"]
4
5   def reserve_resources():
6       my_conf = en.MyProviderConf() \
7           .add_machine(roles=["server"], nodes=3) \
8           .add_machine(roles=["client"], nodes=1)
9       provider = en.MyProvider(my_conf)
10      roles, networks = provider.init()
11      return provider, roles, networks
12
13  def setup_phase(roles):
14      # Install all necessary software on all nodes
15
16  def benchmark_phase(roles):
17      # Run benchmark against the system and collect results
18      en.run_command("./benchmark.sh", roles=roles["client"])
19
20  def run_experiment_with_emulation(roles, latency):
21      # Install and setup all software
22      setup_phase(roles)
23
24      # Apply network emulation: all nodes will have the
25      # same latency for outgoing packets.
26      netem = en.Netem()
27      netem.add_constraints(f"delay {latency}", roles["server"],
28          symmetric=False)
29      netem.deploy()
30      netem.validate()
31
32      # Run experiment
33      results = benchmark_phase(roles)
34
35      # Save results
36      with open(f"results/{latency}/output.csv", "w") as f:
37          ...
38
39      # Deconfigure resources before next iteration
40      netem.destroy()
41
42
43  # Main program
44  for latency in LATENCIES:
45      # We reserve and release resources for each iteration.
46      # This is costly but ensures no side-effect.
47      provider, roles, networks = reserve_resources()
48      run_experiment_with_emulation(roles, latency)
49      provider.destroy()
```

5 Multi-site Experiment on Grid'5000

We deploy the use-case from Sect. 3 on multiple Grid'5000 sites (Fig. 9). This is conceptually similar to a multi-provider experiment, but it is a bit simpler on two key aspects: bidirectional network connectivity between the sites is ensured, and we can use the same authentication method to access resources on both sites. Section 6 will extend the experiment to an actual multi-provider context.

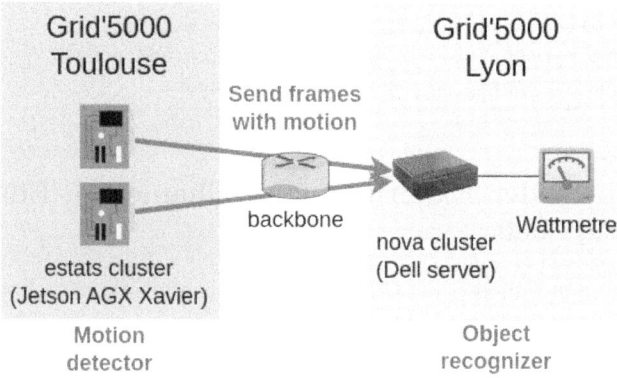

Fig. 9. Multi-site deployment of the use-case on Grid'5000.

We will use two Grid'5000 clusters:

- estats[5] in Toulouse, a cluster with 12 Nvidia AGX Xavier devices. These are small but very capable ARM64 devices, similar to a higher-end Raspberry Pi with an integrated GPU.
- nova[6] in Lyon, a cluster with very standard x86_64 Dell servers. Any other cluster would also work, but this one has the advantage of being energy-monitored with physical wattmetres.

To deploy the application, we rely on Kubernetes, and specifically the K3s Service provided by EnOSlib. It allows to easily deploy K3S clusters on the nodes of the experiment. Anticipating the multi-provider experiment, we deploy two different Kubernetes clusters: first for the edge location, which will run the Motion Detector Application, and then for the cloud location, which will run the Object Recognizer as well as system monitoring services. Listing 1.4 shows how this is done with EnOSlib.

---

[5] https://www.grid5000.fr/w/Toulouse:Hardware#estats.
[6] https://www.grid5000.fr/w/Lyon:Hardware#nova.

Listing 1.4. Simplified code for deploying two K3S clusters (edge and cloud)

```
import enoslib as en


def videoprocessing_setup(roles):
    # Deploy two different Kubernetes cluster
    k3s_edge = en.K3s(master=roles["edge"][0], agent=roles["edge"])
    k3s_edge.deploy()
    k3s_cloud = en.K3s(master=roles["cloud"][0], agent=roles["cloud"])
    k3s_cloud.deploy()
    # Copy Kubernetes deployment files to remote nodes.
    # Adapt deployment files to point to service addresses.
    # Run "kubectl apply" commands on master nodes.
```

6 Multi-provider Experiment on Chameleon Edge and Grid'5000

We extend the experiment: instead of running on multiple sites from the same testbed, we now run an experiment spanning multiple testbeds. We deploy the Motion Detector on Jetson Nano devices from CHI@Edge [14] (CHameleon Infrastructure at Edge), while still deploying the main server in Grid'5000. This deployment is illustrated in Fig. 10 while a simplified code for the deployment is show in Listing 1.5.

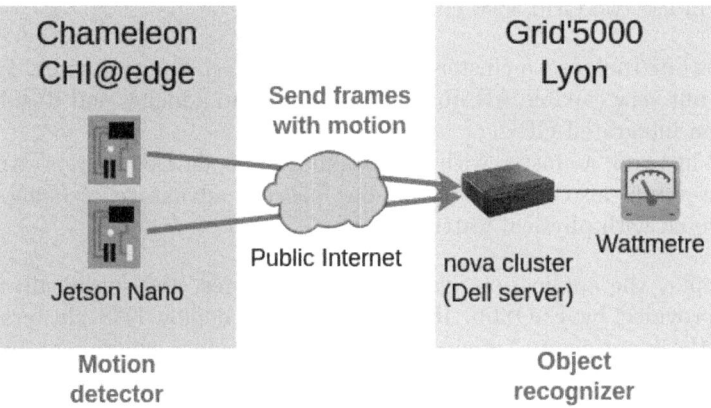

Fig. 10. Multi-provider deployment of the use-case on Chameleon Edge (CHI@EDGE) and Grid'5000.

One of the challenges in multi-testbed experiments is network interconnection. In our case, the Motion Detector in CHI@Edge needs to be able to send data to the Object Recognizer in Grid'5000. There are several possible ways to handle this challenge:

Listing 1.5. Simplified code for multi-provider deployment of the use-case

```
import enoslib as en

chiedge_conf = {
    "walltime": "2:00:00",
    "lease_name": "enoslib-chiedge-lease",
    "resources": {
        "machines": [{
            "roles": ["edge"],
            "device_name": "iot-jetson09",
            "container": {
                "name": "cli-container",
                # This needs to be an ARM64 image
                "image": "debian:12",
            },
        }]
    }
}
g5k_conf = {
    "walltime": "2:00:00",
    "job_name": "enoslib-g5k-job",
    "resources": {
        "machines": [{
            "roles": ["cloud"],
            "cluster": "nova",
            "nodes": 1,
        }]
    }
}
chiedge = en.ChameleonEdge(en.ChameleonEdgeConf.from_dictionary(chiedge_conf))
g5k = en.G5k(en.G5kConf.from_dictionary(g5k_conf))
roles, networks = en.Providers([g5k, chiedge])
```

Native IP Connectivity. If all testbeds have public IP addresses (e.g. using IPv6), nodes can communicate directly with IP over the public Internet. On Grid'5000, IPv6 access is behind a firewall by default, but it can be opened on-demand using the Reconfigurable Firewall service[7]. This is show-cased in another tutorial involving Grid'5000 and FIT IoT-LAB[8].

Native L2 Connectivity. Some network-oriented testbeds such as FABRIC [5] offer advanced network services, including layer-2 connectivity between testbeds. Since this is somewhat complex to setup and only works if testbeds are already

---
[7] https://www.grid5000.fr/w/Reconfigurable_Firewall
[8] https://discovery.gitlabpages.inria.fr/enoslib/jupyter/fit_and_g5k/01_networking.html.

interconnected, this is mostly designed for network-focused experiments that really require layer-2 connectivity.

Tunneling. The last resort is often to use tunnels, such as a Wireguard VPN or SSH-based tunneling. This does not give any guarantees on performance, but can provide basic connectivity.

Chameleon Cloud does not support IPv6, while Grid'5000 provides no public IPv4 addresses on nodes. As a result, the experiment relies on tunneling as a last resort.

7 Conclusion

Since its initial development in 2016, EnOSlib has reached a level of maturity and has been used in many different experiments and projects. At the same time, new features are added regularly to make it easier to perform new kind of distributed experiments.

Among the new features, native multi-provider support is a key enabler for working on the edge-to-cloud continuum. When performing experiments, resources are heterogeneous, are located very far apart, and are often using different infrastructure management software: this makes it difficult to simply obtain simultaneous access on all resources, let alone execute code on all these resources to orchestrate an experiment. The tutorial illustrates how to orchestrate a multi-testbed experiment through a use-case involving communication between edge nodes and cloud nodes. The experiment is deployed on both Grid'5000 in France and Chameleon CHI@Edge in the US.

Acknowledgement. Development of EnOSlib was initially supported by Inria and Orange Labs in the context of the Discovery Open Science initiative. The software is maintained by a core team from Inria on Gitlab (https://gitlab.inria.fr/discovery/enoslib) and receives contributions from many external contributors: over the years, 34 individual contributors have committed code in the git repository. The authors would like to thank all EnOSlib contributors for their work, as well as all users for their precious feedback to help improve the software.

Some experiments were carried out using the Grid'5000 testbed, supported by a scientific interest group hosted by Inria and including CNRS, RENATER and several Universities as well as other organizations.

Some experiments were obtained using the Chameleon testbed supported by the National Science Foundation. We thank the Chameleon team for allowing access to the authors to help develop and test EnOSlib on their infrastructure.

References

1. hubblo-org/scaphandre, April 2025. https://github.com/hubblo-org/scaphandre. original-date: 2020-10-16T14:10:05Z
2. SLICES (scientific large scale infrastructure for computing/communication experimental studies) (2025). https://slices-ri.eu. Accessed 24 Apr 2025

3. Adjih, C., et al.: FIT IoT-LAB: a large scale open experimental IoT testbed. In: 2015 IEEE 2nd World Forum on Internet of Things (WF-IoT), pp. 459–464 (Dec 2015). https://doi.org/10.1109/WF-IoT.2015.7389098, https://ieeexplore.ieee.org/abstract/document/7389098
4. Amaral, M., et al.: Kepler: a framework to calculate the energy consumption of containerized applications. In: 2023 IEEE 16th International Conference on Cloud Computing (CLOUD), pp. 69–71 , July 2023. https://doi.org/10.1109/CLOUD60044.2023.00017, https://ieeexplore.ieee.org/abstract/document/10254956, iSSN: 2159-6190
5. Baldin, I., et al.: FABRIC: A National-Scale Programmable Experimental Network Infrastructure. IEEE Internet Comput. **23**(6), 38–47 (2019). https://doi.org/10.1109/MIC.2019.2958545, https://ieeexplore.ieee.org/abstract/document/8972790
6. Balouek, D., et al.: Adding virtualization capabilities to the Grid'5000 testbed. In: Ivanov, I.I., van Sinderen, M., Leymann, F., Shan, T. (eds.) CLOSER 2012. CCIS, vol. 367, pp. 3–20. Springer, Cham (2013). https://doi.org/10.1007/978-3-319-04519-1_1
7. Balouek-Thomert, D., Rodero, I., Parashar, M.: Evaluating policy-driven adaptation on the edge-to-cloud continuum. In: 2021 IEEE/ACM HPC for Urgent Decision Making (UrgentHPC), pp. 11–20 (2021). https://doi.org/10.1109/UrgentHPC54802.2021.00007
8. Cherrueau, R.A., et al.: Enoslib: a library for experiment-driven research in distributed computing. IEEE Trans. Parallel Distrib. Syst. **33**(6), 1464–1477 (2021). https://doi.org/10.1109/TPDS.2021.3111159
9. Courageux-Sudan, C., Orgerie, A.C., Quinson, M.: Studying the end-to-end performance, energy consumption and carbon footprint of fog applications. In: 2024 IEEE Symposium on Computers and Communications (ISCC), pp. 1–7 (2024). https://doi.org/10.1109/ISCC61673.2024.10733735
10. Delamare, S., Nussbaum, L.: Kwollect: metrics collection for experiments at scale. In: IEEE INFOCOM 2021 - IEEE Conference on Computer Communications Workshops (INFOCOM WKSHPS). pp. 1–6, May 2021. https://doi.org/10.1109/INFOCOMWKSHPS51825.2021.9484540, https://ieeexplore.ieee.org/abstract/document/9484540
11. Fieni, G., Acero, D.R., Rust, P., Rouvoy, R.: PowerAPI: a python framework for building software-defined power meters. J. Open Source Softw. **9**(98), 6670 (2024). https://doi.org/10.21105/joss.06670, https://hal.science/hal-04601379
12. Guilloteau, Q., Bleuzen, J., Poquet, M., Richard, O.: Painless transposition of reproducible distributed environments with Nixos compose. In: 2022 IEEE International Conference on Cluster Computing (CLUSTER), pp. 1–12 (2022). https://doi.org/10.1109/CLUSTER51413.2022.00051
13. Hasenburg, J., Grambow, M., Bermbach, D.: MockFog 2.0: automated execution of fog application experiments in the cloud. IEEE Trans. Cloud Comput. **11**, 58–70 (2021)
14. Keahey, K., et al.: Chameleon@ Edge Community Workshop Report (2021)
15. Keahey, K., et al.: Lessons Learned from the Chameleon Testbed, pp. 219–233 (2020). https://www.usenix.org/conference/atc20/presentation/keahey
16. Kp, G., Pierre, G., Rouvoy, R.: Studying the energy consumption of stream processing engines in the cloud. In: 2023 IEEE International Conference on Cloud Engineering (IC2E), pp. 99–106 (2023). https://doi.org/10.1109/IC2E59103.2023.00019

17. Lambert, T., Ibrahim, S., Jain, T., Guyon, D.: Stragglers' detection in big data analytic systems: The impact of heartbeat arrival. In: 2022 22nd IEEE International Symposium on Cluster, Cloud and Internet Computing (CCGrid), pp. 747–751 (2022). https://doi.org/10.1109/CCGrid54584.2022.00084
18. Mokhtari, A., Jonglez, B., Ledoux, T.: Towards digital sustainability: involving cloud users as key players. In: 2024 IEEE International Conference on Cloud Engineering (IC2E), pp. 126–132 (2024). https://doi.org/10.1109/IC2E61754.2024.00021
19. Noureddine, A.: PowerJoular and JoularJX: multi-platform software power monitoring tools. In: 18th International Conference on Intelligent Environments. Biarritz, France, June 2022. https://doi.org/10.1109/IE54923.2022.9826760, https://hal.science/hal-03608223
20. Philippe, J., Omond, A., Coullon, H., Prud'Homme, C., Raïs, I.: Fast choreography of cross-devops reconfiguration with ballet: a multi-site openstack case study. In: 2024 IEEE International Conference on Software Analysis, Evolution and Reengineering (SANER). IEEE Computer Society, Rovaniemi, Finland, March 2024. https://doi.org/10.1109/SANER60148.2024.00007
21. Rac, S., Sanyal, R., Brorsson, M.: A cloud-edge continuum experimental methodology applied to a 5g core study (2023). https://arxiv.org/abs/2301.11128
22. Rosendo, D., et al.: Provlight: efficient workflow provenance capture on the edge-to-cloud continuum. In: 2023 IEEE International Conference on Cluster Computing (CLUSTER), pp. 221–233 (2023). https://doi.org/10.1109/CLUSTER52292.2023.00026
23. Rosendo, D., Silva, P., Simonin, M., Costan, A., Antoniu, G.: E2clab: exploring the computing continuum through repeatable, replicable and reproducible edge-to-cloud experiments. In: 2020 IEEE International Conference on Cluster Computing (CLUSTER), pp. 176–186 (2020). https://doi.org/10.1109/CLUSTER49012.2020.00028

Mitigating Cryptographic Bottlenecks of Low-Latency BFT Protocols

Pierre-Louis Aublin[1(✉)] and Arne Vogel[2]

[1] IIJ Research Laboratory, Tokyo, Japan
pierrelouis@iij.ad.jp
[2] FAU Erlangen-Nürnberg, Erlangen, Germany
vogel@cs.fau.de

Abstract. Byzantine fault-tolerant protocols enable applications to run even in the presence of arbitrary faults. Unfortunately, to reach a consensus on the order to execute client requests, these protocols perform costly cryptographic operations that limit their performance. This hinders their adoption for latency-sensitive applications executed in data-centres, such as fault-tolerant machine learning or finance applications.

We propose two mechanisms to reduce the impact of digital signature verification: `Speculative Execution` to decouple consensus from the verification of the digital signature of protocol messages; and `Secure Request Broadcast` where replicas do not need to wait for the primary before they can verify a request signature. Both mechanisms are combined with a `Blocklisting` mechanism to ensure robustness against attacks.

We implement both mechanisms in SPECULOR, a PBFT-based BFT protocol tailored for a relaxed fault model where clients do not crash and periodically retransmit their requests. Our evaluation shows SPECULOR reduces the tail-latency by at least 34% compared to PBFT while maintaining robustness under attacks. Finally, we discuss future modifications in order to apply this design to a wide range of BFT protocols under traditional assumptions.

Keywords: Byzantine Fault-Tolerance · digital signature · data-centre

1 Introduction

Byzantine Fault-Tolerance (BFT) offers a powerful promise to modern distributed systems: the ability to maintain functionality even under adverse conditions. Applications can continue to operate reliably despite the presence of faults, malicious behaviours, misconfigurations, and other unpredictable issues.

Data-centre applications require robust fault tolerance and low latency to ensure reliable and efficient operation, even under (Byzantine) failures [22]. This is particularly true in domains such as cloud-provider services, machine learning, and finance. (1) With Blockchain as a Service (BaaS) [5,17], cloud providers propose the basic infrastructure to build scalable and robust blockchain-based applications. (2) Low latency is crucial for real-time predictions and model training of machine learning workloads, while fault tolerance safeguards against data loss and ensures uninterrupted processing [26,29]. (3) Financial applications demand low latency to execute transactions swiftly while fault tolerance is paramount to prevent data corruption [28,31].

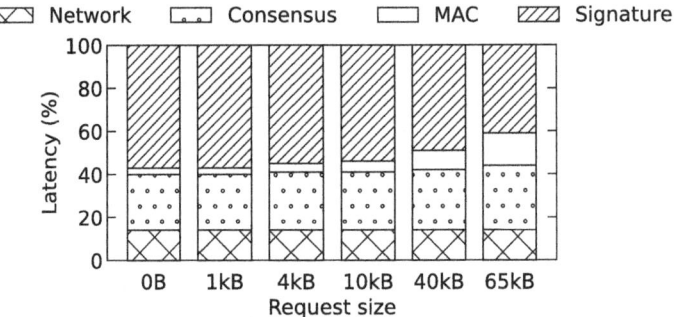

Fig. 1. PBFT latency breakdown ($f = 1$)

Unfortunately, BFT protocols are costly to execute. One reason is the use of cryptographic primitives, in particular digital signatures. They provide strong security guarantees, but are a major performance bottleneck: Fig. 1 shows verifying the client request signature accounts for as much as half the total latency (see Sect. 6.2 for the experimental settings). As described in Sect. 4, digital signatures are necessary to prevent devastating attacks from malicious clients.

In this paper we introduce **Speculative Ordering**, a novel BFT protocol design aimed at data-centre applications that decouples client requests' signature verification and ordering: replicas order the request in parallel of request signature verification. All requests are ordered, but only the correct ones are executed once the signature has been correctly verified.

In addition, we propose a **Secure Broadcast** mechanism resistant to attacks from malicious clients sending their requests only to a subset of the replicas or a malicious primary forging requests. The client signature is computed on a hash of the request and both are included in the PrePrepare message (sent by the replica to propose the next request ordering). Replicas can thus verify the request announced in a PrePrepare without having received it fully.

Speculative Ordering and Secure Broadcast alone are vulnerable to several attacks by malicious clients or replicas. For example, ordering requests with invalid signatures slows down the execution of requests from correct clients. To protect against attacks, we propose a **blocklisting** mechanism: nodes (clients or replicas) become blocklisted if they send invalid requests: their future messages are dropped without further consideration.

We present SPECULOR, a PBFT-based protocol [13] based on the above ideas, in Sect. 5. SPECULOR is tailored for a relaxed fault model where clients never crash and periodically retransmit their requests until execution (see Sect. 3). The reason behind this choice is three-fold: (i) BFT protocols are inherently complex to design. Making this assumption simplifies the initial design exploration; (ii) relaxing the fault model allows us to show the maximal performance benefit of our idea; and (iii) one could argue that a client who does not crash is equivalent to a client who crashes but recovers and resends its request until it gets a response, thus preserving the protocol liveness.

We evaluate SPECULOR in Sect. 6. Compared to PBFT, SPECULOR reduces the tail-latency by up to 34% while keeping performance degradation under attacks below 10%.

We also discuss SPECULOR limitations with our relaxed fault model and how it could be extended to other BFT protocols (see Sect. 7). Other sections include related work (see Sect. 2), problem statement (see Sect. 4), and conclusion (see Sect. 8).

Code Availability. SPECULOR code and artifacts are publicly available at https://zenodo.org/records/15186390.

2 Related Work

Speculation. The concept of introducing speculation to improve the performance of a BFT protocol is not a novel per se. The novelty lies in where speculation is applied. E.g., Zyzzyva [21] introduced speculative *Execution*: replicas optimistically execute client requests proposed by the primary without executing the expensive 3-phase commit. Speculative execution protocols offer better performance than PBFT in the fault-free case, but are vulnerable to attacks [7,14].

Eve [20] first executes client requests, then executes the three-phase commit. This allows Eve to execute client requests in parallel. Eve rollbacks to sequential execution in case of conflicts.

COP [9] parallelizes the consensus: it executes multiple consensus in parallel, leveraging multicore machines, and can reach million of requests ordered per second. However, the authors do not consider failures and, in particular, client requests are not signed.

Advanced Hardware. uBFT [2] offers low-latency BFT for data-centres applications. Similar to speculative execution protocols, it combines an optimistic fast path in the fault-free case and a slow path using signatures upon failures. However, it relies on specific hardware, in particular disaggregated memory and trusted components.

Some recent network cards can encrypt/decrypt network traffic at line-rate speed [23,25]. However, to the best of our knowledge they cannot process digital signatures at dozens of Gbps. Even more, Bravo et al. [10] observed that *"contrary to anecdotal evidence, hardware accelerators for cryptographic operations alone will not result in significantly better performance"*.

Alternatives to Digital Signatures. Matrix signatures [3] offer non-repudiation without digital signatures. However, they require complex changes, non-trivial key management, additional communication rounds between replicas, and are vulnerable to some complex timing attacks.

Aguilera et al. recently proposed DSig [1], a digital signature system that achieves microsecond performance for data-centres. Based on the observation that nodes in a data-centre know each others, DSig combines slow traditional signatures with fast hash-based signatures. The authors have applied DSig to speed up inter-replicas communication and have not considered faulty behaviours.

Summary. In contrast to the above works, we aim to propose solution that improves existing BFT protocols performance without sacrificing robustness, the need to fall back to a slower execution path, or the need for specialized hardware.

3 Fault Model

The system is composed of $n = 3f+1$ replicas, among which at most f are faulty, and c clients, among which an arbitrary number can be faulty. Faulty nodes, replicas or clients, behave in any arbitrary way in accordance to the Byzantine failure model. Furthermore, we assume clients (both correct and malicious) do not crash and periodically retransmit their requests until they are executed.

All messages, both exchanged with clients and other replicas, are authenticated with a Message Authentication Code (MAC), which uses a secret cryptographic key to authenticate a message between two nodes known only by these two (e.g.a client and a replica). Client requests also include a digital signature, based on asymmetric cryptography, that provides the non-repudiation property. We assume cryptographic operations to be correctly implemented and resistant against attacks; in particular malicious nodes cannot create a valid MAC or signature for another node without being in possession of their key and checksum operations are collision-resistant.

We make the standard assumption of an eventually synchronous network: after an arbitrary period of time, the network behaves synchronously, i.e., communication latency is bounded [11]. We also assume messages are retransmitted until delivered as the network can reorder, drop or modify network packets.

Flooding attacks, where clients or replicas send invalid messages as fast as they can, are out of scope. Existing solutions [8,14] offer some degree of protection.

4 Problem Statement

For a successful deployment in a data-centre, BFT protocols require both (i) low end-to-end latency (i.e.the latency observed by clients); and (ii) robustness, that is to say they are able to deliver the replicated service despite adverse conditions while minimizing performance degradation. We show in this section these requirements are currently not met.

4.1 Signature Verification

Signature verification[1] is one of BFT protocols performance bottlenecks [4]: it takes up to 50% of PBFT end-to-end latency as shown in Fig. 1 (we refer the reader to Sect. 6.2 for the experimental settings). Even when increasing the number of tolerated faults to $f = 10$, hence the number of replicas to $n = 31$, signature verification still accounts for more than 24% of the end-to-end latency.

As shown by Clement et al. [14], signatures are necessary: without them, PBFT is vulnerable to attacks from malicious clients: if a single malicious client creates a malformed request valid for only a subset of the replicas, replicas will trigger a view change. If it keeps sending malformed requests, the protocol will be stuck in a view change loop, unable to process requests from legitimate clients and stopping the protocol execution.

More formally, signatures provide the non-repudiation property, which ensures that if one correct node validates a message, then all the correct nodes will also validate the same message. Compared to relying on MAC only, correct replicas have the additional guarantee the client request they validate will also be validated by other correct replicas.

4.2 Request Dissemination

If all replicas could start verifying client signatures as soon as possible, end-to-end latency would be reduced. To the best of our knowledge, in all BFT protocols where client requests are signed, replicas receive the request from the primary only after it has himself received the request, verified it, and sent a PrePrepare. One idea is for the clients to send their requests to all replicas, and replicas to verify all the requests they receive, regardless of whether they have received the corresponding PrePrepare or not.

Some protocols already implement such a request dissemination scheme. Unfortunately (i) a description of the mechanism is often omitted [18,30]; (ii) it adds extra communication rounds [6,8] or waiting phase [13], and thus extra latency; or (iii) it has not been evaluated under faults [18,30].

We consider PBFT broadcast mechanism as an illustration. A client sends a Request to all replicas. The primary verifies the client signature, then creates and sends a PrePrepare containing only the Request hash. Follower replicas send a Prepare message only if they have already received the request from the client; otherwise they do nothing [12].

If a malicious client sends its request only to the primary, follower replicas will not be able to send a Prepare message, thus stalling the protocol execution. While they will eventually initiate a view change, the malicious client can stop the protocol execution by indefinitely repeating this attack.

---

[1] On our evaluation platform, signature creation is faster than verification: $22\,\mu S$ compared to $60\,\mu s$ with ED25519.

5 SPECULOR

We propose SPECULOR, a novel BFT protocol design that reduces the performance impact of signature verification in BFT protocols while still maintaining robustness, i.e., gracious performance degradation in case of adverse conditions.

SPECULOR **decouples client request ordering from its verification** (Sect. 5.1). Without signature verification on the critical path anymore, end-to-end latency perceived by clients is improved. To achieve this goal without compromising its performance under attack, SPECULOR embeds two additional mechanisms: **secure request broadcast** (Sect. 5.2) and **blocklisting of malicious nodes** (Sect. 5.3).

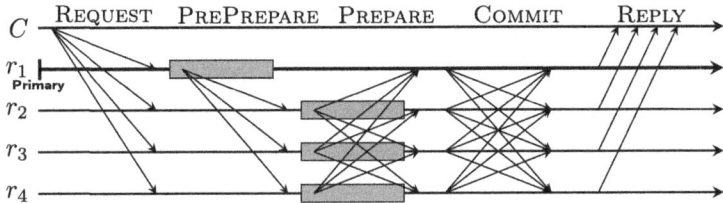

Fig. 2. SPECULOR consensus in the fault-free case ($f = 1$; the box indicates signature verification)

Figure 2 gives the intuition of SPECULOR latency benefits when applied to PBFT: client request verification is not on the critical path anymore, but done in parallel of the consensus, and replicas do not need to wait for the primary before they verify a request signature.

At a high-level, SPECULOR combines: (see Fig. 3): (i) the original BFT protocol, in charge of client request ordering; (ii) the signature verifier, in charge of verifying signatures; (iii) the MAC verifier, which ensures the BFT protocol receives only messages free of corruption and sent by a valid node; (iv) the network module, which sends and receives messages to/from the underlying network stack; and (v) the blocklisting module, in charge of early dropping messages coming from blocklisted nodes so that they do not negatively impact the system performance.

When a replica receives a message, the blocklisting module first checks whether the sender is blocklisted or not ①. If not, the message can be received by the network layer and its MAC is verified ②. If invalid, e.g.due to corruption during transmission or a malicious action, the message is dropped. If valid, the message is simultaneously sent to the BFT protocol and signature verifier ③ (in case of a signed client request). Once the signature verification result is available, it is transmitted to the BFT protocol to complete or discard the consensus certificate ④. If verification fails, the signature verifier asks the blocklisting module to blocklist the sender ⑤.

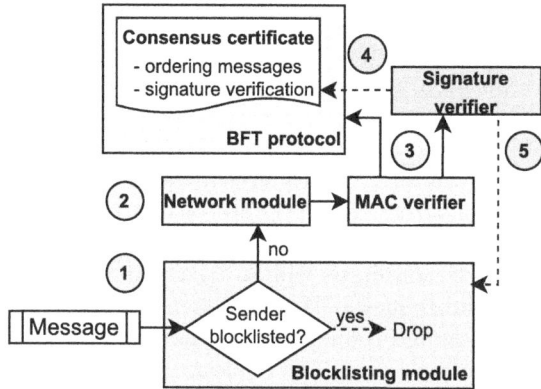

Fig. 3. Overview of SPECULOR at a replica. Solid lines illustrate message flow while dashed lines illustrate logical flow.

SPECULOR changes the underlying BFT protocol only slightly: (i) SPECULOR tracks the result of client requests signature verification; (ii) SPECULOR provides a new protocol to ask missing requests from the primary and manages several related timers; (iii) SPECULOR manages a blocklist mechanism; and (iv) SPECULOR replicas include pending consensus and requests in the view change messages to ensure liveness. Other components of the BFT protocol, such as the different messages structure and state management, remain untouched.

We detail below each contribution of SPECULOR. Pseudocode can be found in the appendix at the end of the paper.

5.1 SPECULative ORdering

SPECULOR main novel idea is *Speculative Ordering*, where a client request is ordered in parallel to its signature verification. In existing protocols, signature verification is performed on the critical path: a request is ordered only after its signature verification has succeeded. Said in another way, a consensus certificate always refers to a valid request. In contrast, in SPECULOR a request is ordered without taking into account its signature validity. The only verification performed on the critical path is the inexpensive MAC check (see Fig. 1) to ensure the message content has not been corrupted and its sender is legitimate.

When the signature verifier module receives a request, it checks whether it has already received it. If not, it assigns it a Pending verification status, meaning the request signature has not been verified yet, and asynchronously verifies it.

In parallel of signature verification, the primary creates and sends the PrePrepare. Then, replicas receive the PrePrepare, asynchronously check the request it contains, and create and send the Prepare.

SPECULOR replicas can create a consensus for a request whose signature is invalid. Even if the consensus is *complete*, that is to say the ordering messages have been gathered (1 PrePrepare, $2f$ Prepare, and $2f + 1$ Commit in PBFT), replicas cannot immediately execute the request, but need to check its signature validity. Thus, SPECULOR augments the consensus certificate with the result of the signature verification.

A replica executes a request if and only if the consensus certificate is complete, it is in possession of the request, and the request signature is valid. If the request is missing, the replica will ask the primary. If the request signature is invalid, this consensus can be ignored and the protocol moves to the next one. If the request signature is pending, signature verification is still in progress.

With SPECULOR, A consensus will be triggered for requests whose signature is invalid (i.e.invalid requests). These consensuses are completed after the traditional message exchange rounds, but do not lead to an execution. They hinder the progression of correct clients' requests and degrade the system performance. To counter this attack, SPECULOR introduces a Blocklisting mechanism (see Sect. 5.3).

5.2 Secure Request Broadcast

SPECULOR introduce a novel *Secure request Broadcast* scheme so that replicas do not need to wait for the `prePrepare` message before they receive the request. Compared to prior works (see Sect. 4), our mechanism takes into account malicious behaviours from both clients or replicas.

Secure Broadcast makes the following changes: (i) the request signature is computed on a hash of the message instead of directly on the message content (this hash is the one included in the `PrePrepare`); and (ii) the primary now includes in the `PrePrepare` both the request hash and its signature. With these two changes, it becomes possible to detect whether an invalid request has been forged by a malicious primary or sent by a malicious client, by comparing the request metadata in the `PrePrepare` with the full request[2].

A client request signature is verified at most once. If the replica receives a `Request` before it receives its corresponding `PrePrepare`, then it will verify the signature at this stage. Conversely, if the replica receives a request metadata in a `PrePrepare` before the full request has been received, then it checks its signature at that stage.

A replica might have received a request metadata in a `PrePrepare` before its corresponding request by the time it is ready to execute the request. This can happen if the network is slow or if a malicious client sends its request to only a subset of the replicas. SPECULOR introduces a *Request Inquiry* mechanism and two timeouts: (i) `client_req_timeout`, how long a replica has been waiting for a request from the client (i.e.it has received its metadata in a `PrePrepare`); and (ii) `primary_req_timeout`, how long a replica has been waiting from the primary for a missing request.

When a replica trying to execute a consensus misses its request, it starts a timer for this request hash and sends a `RequestInquiry` message to the primary. The primary has sent a `PrePrepare` for this request and should possess it.

---

[2] The `PrePrepare` also includes the client ID so that the correct signature key will be used during verification.

Upon receiving a `RequestInquiry`, the primary sends back an `Inquiry Answer` with the full request. Upon reception, the replica checks whether the received request and hashes match. If not, it triggers a view change as the primary sent an unrelated request and request hash.

Replicas periodically check for expired timers. First, if, for a given request, its `client_req_timeout` elapsed time is greater than `CLIENT_TIMEOUT_MS` (set to the maximal latency between clients and replicas), then the replica inquires the primary for the request: the replica has received a corresponding `PrePrepare`, but no request from the client yet. Second, if, for a given request, its `primary_req_timeout` elapsed time is greater than `PRIMARY_INQUIRY_TIMEOUT_MS` (empirically set to 2∗`CLIENT_TIMEOUT_MS` in our experiments), then the replica initiates a view change: neither the primary nor client could provide the request[3].

Malicious clients could slow down the protocol by sending their requests to the primary only, forcing replicas to execute the request inquiry protocol. SPECULOR prevents this attack with its blocklisting mechanism presented in the next section.

5.3 Blocklist

Alone, Speculative Ordering and Secure request Broadcast are vulnerable to a malicious attacker trying to reduce system performance. In Speculative Ordering, malicious clients sending invalid requests will trigger many consensus not leading to an execution, slowing down the consensus of correct clients. In Secure request Broadcast, malicious clients could send their requests only to the primary, forcing correct replicas to inquire them to the primary.

To alleviate these problems, SPECULOR implements a *Blocklisting mechanism*. If a correct replica detects that a node, either client or replica, acts maliciously, then it will add this node to a blocklist, dropping future received messages. Similar to Aardvark [14] the node is blocklisted for an arbitrary period of time. Techniques such as rejuvenation [15,24,27] can be leveraged to add a new fresh node into the system.

Some attacks, such as a malicious client sending requests with a spoofed client ID, would not trigger blocklisting: it is not possible to determine whether the client is malicious or the message has been corrupted.

Replicas maintain a blocklist state information. Each node is in one of the three following states: `Allowlisted` (by default), `Suspected` or `Blocklisted`. When a node does a malicious action, such as sending a request with an invalid signature, it becomes `Suspected`. Due to Speculative Ordering, a replica can receive a `PrePrepare` containing a request with an invalid signature, because the primary has sent it before the completion of signature verification. If a `Suspected` node continues to act maliciously, it will eventually be `Blocklisted`.

---

[3] All messages, including request inquiries, are periodically retransmitted to cope with message loss.

Finally, after an arbitrary period of time, a blocklisted node can be `Allowlisted`, assuming it has been repaired.

The blocklisting rules are as follows. First, if request signature verification fails for a given client, then it is immediately `Blocklisted`. If the request has been received from a `PrePrepare`, the primary state moves to `Suspected`, or `Blocklisted` if it was already suspected and has sent another request from the same client which has already sent an invalid request previously. In SPECULOR, consensus instances do not overlap: the primary waits for the completion of a consensus before sending the next `PrePrepare`. This prevents a malicious client getting the primary blacklisted by sending invalid requests in quick succession.

Second, replicas (including the primary) monitor how many `RequestInquiry` they send/receive. Compared to counting `RequestInquiry` only at the primary, doing it at every replica makes SPECULOR robust against a malicious client colluding with a malicious primary. If, for a particular client, a replica records more than the average number of inquiries per client, then it blocklists this client: it obviously experiences some failure, either network connection is of poor quality or it is malicious and sends its requests only to the primary.

5.4 Implementation

We have implemented SPECULOR in 3000 LoC (Lines of Code) of Rust. Speculative Ordering is implemented in 100 LoC, Secure request Broadcast in 200 LoC, and blocklisting takes less than 100 LoC. Messages are exchanged via UDP and contain a HMAC with SHA256. Signatures are generated/verified with ED25519 [19] by a set of *Cryptographic threads*.

The blocklisting mechanism adds a rule in the `iptables` OS firewall to drop messages from the sender via its IP and port as soon as they reach the node.

SPECULOR batches the `PrePrepare`, `RequestInquiry` and `InquiryAnswer` messages to improve performance. Instead of sending one message per request, replicas include several requests into the same message.

6 Evaluation

We evaluate the robustness and performance of SPECULOR under various conditions. Our main results show: (i) SPECULOR provides defenses against a wide-range of malicious behaviours (Sect. 6.1); (ii) SPECULOR improves PBFT throughput by up to $3x$ and reduces its tail latency by 34% (Sect. 6.3); (iii) SPECULOR throughput degrades by at most 10% (Sect. 6.4).

6.1 Security Discussion

This section lists various attacks from malicious clients or replicas and describes SPECULOR countermeasures.

Invalid Request Signature. A malicious client sends requests with an invalid signature. The primary proposes to order its first request while checking its signature. Once the signature validity check has failed, replicas blocklist the client and ignore its subsequent requests. If the primary continues to propose requests from the malicious client, replicas will blocklist it and initiate a view change.

Forged Request. A malicious primary send forged client requests in the `PrePrepare`. Its goal is to blocklist correct clients who supposedly sent the forged request.

First, correct replicas initiate a view change if they receive two invalid requests from the same client in two different `PrePrepare` (See Sect. 5.3). This limits the attack to forging at most one request per client.

Second, correct replicas blocklist clients only after they have received the complete (invalid) request from the client or via a request inquiry to the primary. The request metadata included in the `PrePrepare` is not enough to take a decision regarding if the request was forged or not.

This attack will fail: the malicious primary is limited to only one forged request per client if it wants to stay primary, while the (correct) client will not be blocklisted.

Request Sent to Follower Replicas Only. A malicious client floods follower replicas with valid requests but ignore the primary, to exhaust follower replicas memory.

To prevent this attack, correct replicas bound the maximum number of requests received without a corresponding `PrePrepare`. Replicas also forward such requests to the primary if it has not sent a `PrePrepare` containing these requests by a timeout.

Signature Invalid for a Subset of the Replicas. A malicious client sends the same request but with different signatures to the different replicas with the goal of initiating a view change, e.g., to promote a malicious replica to the role of primary. Either the request sent only to the primary has a valid signature, or the request sent only to the other replicas has a valid signature.

In the first case, the primary creates a `PrePrepare` with a valid signature that will be accepted by correct replicas. Once a correct replica receives the full request, its signature is invalid and the client is blocklisted.

In the second case, the primary creates a `PrePrepare` with an invalid signature it has not checked yet. Due to Speculative Ordering, follower replicas do not blocklist it immediately. Once signature verification at the primary has finished, it will blocklist the malicious client.

Invalid MACs. If a malicious client tries to impersonate another one, its requests will not have a valid MAC as the MAC key is kept private between two nodes (in this case, between the correct client and each of the replicas). However, replicas will not blacklist the sender of these requests as they cannot make the difference between data corruption of the request and an active attack. Keys can be periodically rotated to prevent an attacker reusing a leaked key.

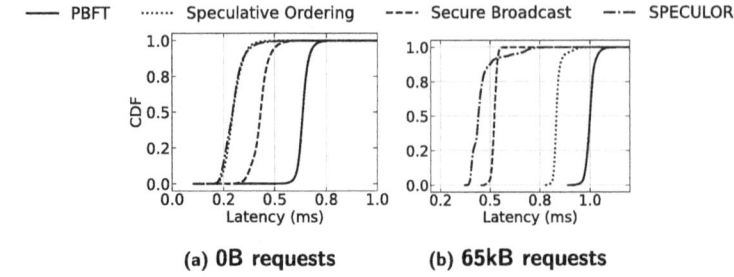

Fig. 4. Cumulative latency, fault-free case

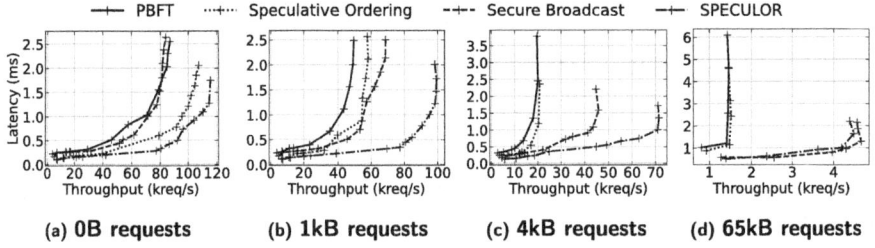

Fig. 5. Latency vs throughput, fault-free case

6.2 Experimental Settings

Experiments are run on the c6525-25g cluster of the Cloudlab experimental platform [16]. Each machine of this cluster is composed of a 16-core AMD 7302P CPU running at 3.00 GHz, 128 GB of RAM, and a Mellanox ConnectX-5 25 Gb NIC. Each machine runs Ubuntu 22.04 and Rust 1.73.

We execute at most one replica per machine; all clients are executed on a single dedicated machine and send their requests as fast as they can in a closed-loop, waiting for the result of a previous request before sending a new one. Unless noted otherwise, f is set to 1 ($n = 4$ replicas); some experiments are run with up to 31 replicas ($f = 10$). There are 12 cryptographic threads (i.e., 12 signatures can be checked in parallel) per replica. The replicated application is single-threaded.

Performance is measured at the clients in terms of throughput and latency. Each experiment is run multiple times to ensure a $< 1\%$ standard deviation.

6.3 Performance in the Fault-Free Case

This section discusses the raw performance of PBFT, Speculative Ordering, Secure request Broadcast and SPECULOR with micro-benchmarks, for requests ranging from 0B to 65kB (the maximum payload size for a single UDP datagram). Reply size is 0B and the maximum number of tolerated faults is fixed to $f = 1$.

Results are reported in Fig. 5. First, SPECULOR latency is between $2.2x$ and $3.1x$ lower than PBFT, respectively from 0.40 ms to 0.18 ms at 24,000 req/s with 1 kB requests, and from 0.46 ms to 0.15 ms at 10,300 req/s with 4 kB requests.

Second, SPECULOR consistently outperforms PBFT for each request size, improving the throughput by at least 33%, from 86,900 req/s to 115,600 reqs/s with 0 B requests, and increases up to $3x$ with 65 kB requests, from 1,400 req/s to 4,400 req/s. Throughput improvement is directly linked to the lower latency: clients spend less time waiting for the result of their requests. As their sending speed is not limited, they can send more requests per time unit, thus improving the overall throughput.

SPECULOR performance improvement is due to the combination of both Speculative Ordering and Secure Broadcast. Up to 1 kB requests, Speculative Ordering is the main contributor to the improved performance, while Secure Broadcast comes into action for requests larger or equal to 4 kB. For example, with 0B requests, Secure Broadcast achieves only 83,800 req/s (3.6% lower than PBFT), while Speculative Ordering achieves 107,400 req/s. On the opposite, with 65 kB requests, Speculative Ordering achieves only 1,500 req/s (7% higher than PBFT), while Secure Broadcast reaches 4,700 req/s.

According to Fig. 1, signature verification with requests larger than 4 kB accounts for at least 37% of the latency, thus we could expect Speculative Ordering to reach a higher throughput. The problem is UDP datagram maximum size limits batching. With 4 kB requests, a batch contains at most 15 requests, while Speculative Ordering maximum throughput is reached with more than 25 clients. This means that every time the primary creates a `PrePrepare`, there are more than 10 pending requests waiting for the next `PrePrepare` before they can be ordered. In contrast, with 0B requests, there are around 20 requests each time the primary creates the `PrePrepare`, but they all fit in a single message.

In a second experiment we measure the latency of each client request. Figure 4 reports the latency distribution with requests of 0 B and 65kB. The number of clients is fixed to respectively 25 (0 B requests) and 1 (65kB requests). As the system is not fully saturated, latency does not include any queueing overhead, showing a clearer difference between the different protocols.

For 0B requests (Fig. 4a), SPECULOR requests are served 53% faster than PBFT requests: on average, 299 ms compared to 638 ms. The 99th percentile is also lower: from 720 ms to 463 ms (-36%). This is primarily due to Speculative Ordering (both SPECULOR and Speculative Ordering cumulative latencies are indistinguishable). Secure Broadcast decreases the average latency by 32% (from 638 ms to 434 ms) and the 99th percentile by 23% (from 720 ms to 553 ms).

For 65 kB requests (Fig. 4a), SPECULOR average latency is 55% lower than PBFT (from 1000 ms to 455 ms), while the 99th percentile is 34% lower (from 1072 ms to 706 ms). With Secure Broadcast, replicas receive (large) requests as soon as possible: Secure Broadcast average latency is 522 ms; the 99th percentile is 552 ms. Compared to PBFT, this represents a 48% decrease. In contrast, Speculative Ordering alone reduces the average latency by only 16% (down to 838 ms) and the 99th percentile by 13% (down to 935 ms).

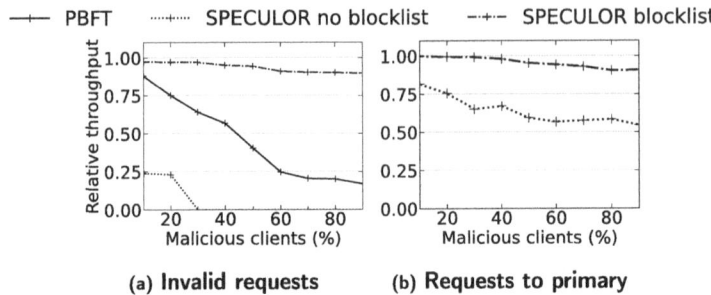

Fig. 6. Throughput degradation under attacks

6.4 Performance Under Attack

This section reports the performance of SPECULOR and PBFT under various attacks. Experiments are executed with $f = 1$, at most 50 clients and 0 B requests, which corresponds to 70,000 req/s. Each Malicious client sends 4,000 req/s, the maximum throughput of a single correct client.

Speculative Ordering. Figure 6a shows the throughput relative to a fault-free execution when some percentage of malicious clients send invalid requests.

PBFT throughput related to a fault-free execution degrades as malicious clients increase, from 0.88 with 10% malicious clients to 0.17 with 90% malicious clients. This is expected: the primary is verifying all requests, including the ones from malicious clients.

SPECULOR without blocklisting is vulnerable to malicious clients: its relative throughput is only 0.24 with 10% malicious clients, and drops to 0 with more than 30% of malicious clients. This is because all replicas verify all requests, including the ones with an invalid signature.

When activating blocklisting, the throughput drops down to at most 90% of the throughput relative to a fault-free execution (90% malicious clients).

Secure Broadcast. In the second attack scenario, a malicious client sends its requests only to the primary. Correct replicas will have to inquire the request to the primary once the consensus is complete, before they can execute the request. As reported in Fig. 6b, the attacker is able to decrease the throughput from 18% (10% malicious clients) to 46% (90%). In comparison, if all clients send their requests only to the primary, the throughput degrades by 70%.

To decrease the effect of this attack, SPECULOR blocklists clients for which replicas inquire requests to the primary more than for other clients on average. With this blocklisting condition, SPECULOR throughput decreases by at most 9% (90% malicious clients).

7 Limitations

7.1 Relaxed Fault Model

We have presented SPECULOR with a relaxed fault model where clients do not crash and periodically retransmit their requests until they are executed. Without this assumption, SPECULOR does not ensure liveness. Specifically, if a request hash is only known to the client and the primary, but no other (correct) replica, SPECULOR can potentially still complete the consensus process for this request hash. If afterward both the client and primary crash, all sources for the full request disappear, meaning the remaining replicas are required to execute a request they will never be able to obtain.

One solution is to introduce a new message exchange round to ensure at least one correct replica is in possession of the request before replicas start ordering it. This is the solution chosen by RBFT [8] or Prime [6]. The downside of this solution is it introduces a new synchronisation point, thus reducing the latency improvement of SPECULOR.

7.2 Generalisation to Other Protocols

In this paper, only the client request is signed. Some protocols such as HotStuff [30], however, digitally sign all messages, including inter-replicas messages. We believe SPECULOR can be generalized to these BFT protocols.

The difficulty with implementing SPECULOR with such protocols lies in the fact that more messages with an invalid signature are in-flight in the system before the culprit can be blocklisted. This increases the attack surface.

7.3 Blocklisting Mechanism

Blocklisting a node for some period of time is an arbitrary solution. Instead, we could introduce a *slow signature verification path* for nodes deemed malicious. Instead of ignoring their messages, replicas could process them when they have time, after processing messages from other nodes. Malicious replicas might take advantage of this slow path to delay processing some client requests. To prevent this, an idea is for correct replicas to reach a consensus on the decision to move a node to the slow path.

8 Conclusion

We presented SPECULOR, a novel BFT protocol improving consensus performance without sacrificing robustness. SPECULOR introduces *Speculative Ordering* to parallelize consensus and request signature verification, specifies *Secure request Broadcast* to securely disseminate client requests to all replicas, and integrates a *Blocklisting* mechanism to thwart various attacks. Evaluation shows applying SPECULOR to PBFT reduces its tail-latency by up to 34% without compromising its performance under attack.

We also discussed SPECULOR limitations in our relaxed fault model. Overall, removing signature verification from the critical path reduces end-to-end-latency, but ensuring the protocol is robust against attacks requires additional message exchanges that will reduce the performance gain. Further work is needed to explore the practical benefit of this idea.

Acknowledgements. We are very grateful to the anonymous reviewers for their helpful comments as well as our colleagues for many fruitful discussions.

Conflicts of Interests. The authors have no competing interests to declare that are relevant to the content of this article.

Appendix: SPECULOR pseudocode

```
1  enum SignatureVerification {
2      Valid, Invalid, Pending,
3  }
4
5  requests: HashMap<HashedRequest, (Request, SignatureVerification)>
6
7  client_req_timeout: HashMap<HashedRequest, Time>
8  primary_req_timeout: HashMap<HashedRequest, Time>
9
10 enum BlockListState {
11     Allowlisted, Blocklisted, Suspected,
12 }
13
14 blocklist_state: HashMap<NodeID, BlockListState>
15 blocklist_inquiries: HashMap<NodeID, NodeID>
16 blocklist_fairness: HashMap<NodeID, NodeID>
17 primary_suspected_for_client: HashSet<NodeID>
```

Listing 1.1. SPECULOR main data structures

```
1  fn verify_request(h: HashedRequest, r: Request) {
2      if !requests.contains(h) {
3          requests[h] = (r, SignatureVerification::Pending);
4          speculatively_verify(h, r);
5      }
6  }
7
8  async fn speculatively_verify(h: HashedRequest, r: Request) {
9      let v = verify_signature(r);
10     requests[h] = (r, if v SignatureVerification::Valid else
                SignatureVerification::Invalid);
11
12     if !v {
13         blocklist_client(r.cid);
```

```
14      if received_in_preprepare(r)
15        suspect_or_blocklist_primary();
16    }
17  }
```

Listing 1.2. SPECULOR signature verifier module

```
1   fn handle_request(h: HashedRequest, r: Request) {
2     if my_id() != primary_id() {
3       client_req_timeout.remove(h);
4       return;
5     }
6
7     let pp = create_new_pp(h, r);
8     send_to_all_replicas(pp);
9   }
10
11  fn handle_preprepare(pp: PrePrepare) {
12    let cid = pp.request_cid;
13    let h = pp.request_hash;
14    let r = create_fake_request_from_hash(cid, h, pp.request_sig);
15
16    if client_is_blocklisted(cid) {
17      view_change();
18      return;
19    }
20
21    if !requests.contains(h) {
22      client_req_timeout[h] = time::now();
23      speculatively_verify(h, r)
24    }
25
26    let p = create_new_prepare(pp);
27    send_to_all_replicas(p);
28  }
29
30  fn try_execute_consensus(c: Consensus) {
31    if !c.is_complete() return;
32
33    let h = c.request_hash;
34    let (r, v) = requests[h];
35    if v == SigVerifState::Invalid seq_num++;
36    else if v == SigVerifState::Valid {
37      if r.is_fake_request() {
38        inquire_request(h);
39      } else {
40        execute_consensus(r);
41        seq_num++;
42      }
43    } else if v == SigVerifState::Pending {
```

```
44      // do nothing
45    }
46  }
```

Listing 1.3. SPECULOR BFT protocol module

```
1   fn inquire_request(cid: NodeID, h: HashedRequest) {
2     let m = RequestInquiry::new(my_id(), h);
3     blocklist_monitor_inquiry(cid);
4     send_message(primary_id(), m);
5     primary_req_timeout[h] = time::now();
6   }
7
8   fn handle_request_inquiry(m: RequestInquiry) {
9     let r = requests[m.h]
10    let a = InquiryAnswer::new(my_id(), (m.h, r));
11    blocklist_monitor_inquiry(r.cid);
12    send_message(m.sender, a);
13  }
14
15  fn handle_inquiry_answer(m: InquiryAnswer) {
16    let (h, r) = m.request;
17    if h != create_request_hash(r) {
18      view_change();
19    } else {
20      primary_req_timeout.remove(h);
21    }
22  }
23
24  fn check_timeouts() {
25    for (h, t) in client_req_timeout.filter(|(h, t)| t.elapsed() >
        CLIENT_TIMEOUT_MS) {
26      let (_, s) = requests[h];
27      client_req_timeout.remove(h);
28      if s != SigVerifState::Invalid {
29        inquire_request(h);
30      }
31    }
32
33    for (h, t) in primary_req_timeout.filter(|(h, t)| t.elapsed() >
        PRIMARY_INQUIRY_TIMEOUT_MS) {
34      view_change();
35      break;
36    }
37  }
```

Listing 1.4. SPECULOR request inquiry protocol

```
1   fn blocklist_client(cid: NodeID) {
2     blocklist_state[cid] = BlockListState::Blocklisted; blocklist(cid);
3   }
```

```
 4
 5  fn suspect_or_blocklist_primary(cid: NodeID) {
 6    let p = primary_id();
 7    let s = blocklist_state[p];
 8    if s == BlockListState::Allowlisted {
 9      blocklist_state[p] = BlockListState::Suspected;
10      primary_suspected_for_client.insert(cid);
11    } else if s == BlockListState::Suspected &&
          primary_suspected_for_client.contains(cid) {
12      blocklist_state[p] = BlockListState::Blocklisted;
13      blocklist(p); view_change();
14    }
15  }
16
17  fn blocklist_monitor_inquiry(cid: NodeID) {
18    let i = ++blocklist_inquiries[cid];
19    let avg = average(blocklist_inquiries);
20    if i > BLOCKLIST_INQUIRIES_RATIO * avg {
21      blocklist_state[cid] = BlockListState::Blocklisted;
22      blocklist(cid);
23    }
24  }
```

Listing 1.5. SPECULOR blocklist mechanism

References

1. Aguilera, M.K., Burgelin, C., Guerraoui, R., Murat, A., Xygkis, A., Zablotchi, I.: Dsig: breaking the barrier of signatures in data centers (2024). https://arxiv.org/abs/2406.07215
2. Aguilera, M.K., et al.: ubft: Microsecond-scale bft using disaggregated memory. In: Proceedings of the 28th ACM International Conference on Architectural Support for Programming Languages and Operating Systems, vol. 2, pp. 862–877 (2023)
3. Aiyer, A.S., Alvisi, L., Bazzi, R.A., Clement, A.: Matrix signatures: from MACs to digital signatures in distributed systems. In: Taubenfeld, G. (ed.) DISC 2008. LNCS, vol. 5218, pp. 16–31. Springer, Heidelberg (2008). https://doi.org/10.1007/978-3-540-87779-0_2
4. Alqahtani, S., Demirbas, M.: Bottlenecks in blockchain consensus protocols. In: IEEE International Conference on Omni-Layer Intelligent Systems (COINS) (2021)
5. Amazon: Amazon Managed Blockchain (2022). https://aws.amazon.com/managed-blockchain/
6. Amir, Y., Coan, B., Kirsch, J., Lane, J.: Prime: byzantine replication under attack. IEEE Trans. Dependable Secure Comput. **8**(4), 564–577 (2010)
7. Aublin, P.L., Guerraoui, R., Knežević, N., Quéma, V., Vukolić, M.: The next 700 bft protocols. ACM Trans. Comput. Syst. (TOCS) **32**(4), 1–45 (2015)

8. Aublin, P.L., Mokhtar, S.B., Quéma, V.: RBFT: redundant byzantine fault tolerance. In: IEEE 33rd International Conference on Distributed Computing Systems (2013)
9. Behl, J., Distler, T., Kapitza, R.: Consensus-oriented parallelization: how to earn your first million. In: Proceedings of the 16th Annual Middleware Conference (2015)
10. Bravo, M., István, Z., Sit, M.K.: Towards improving the performance of bft consensus for future permissioned blockchains. arXiv:2007.12637 (2020)
11. Cachin, C., Guerraoui, R., Rodrigues, L.: Introduction to Reliable and Secure Distributed Programming, 2nd edn. Springer, Heidelberg (2011). https://doi.org/10.1007/978-3-642-15260-3
12. Castro, M., Liskov, B.: Practical byzantine fault tolerance and proactive recovery. ACM Trans. Comput. Syst. (TOCS) **20**(4), 398–461 (2002)
13. Castro, M., Liskov, B., et al.: Practical byzantine fault tolerance. In: OsDI 1999, pp. 173–186 (1999)
14. Clement, A., Wong, E.L., Alvisi, L., Dahlin, M., Marchetti, M.: Making byzantine fault tolerant systems tolerate byzantine faults. In: NSDI, vol. 9, pp. 153–168 (2009)
15. Distler, T., Cachin, C., Kapitza, R.: Resource-efficient byzantine fault tolerance. IEEE Trans. Comput. **65**(9), 2807–2819 (2015)
16. Duplyakin, D., et al.: The design and operation of CloudLab. In: Proceedings of the USENIX Annual Technical Conference (ATC), pp. 1–14 (2019). https://www.flux.utah.edu/paper/duplyakin-atc19
17. Gaël Blanchemain: Azure BaaS (2018). https://docs.nethereum.com/en/latest/azure/set-up-blockchain-on-azure/
18. Giridharan, N., Suri-Payer, F., Abraham, I., Alvisi, L., Crooks, N.: Motorway: seamless high speed bft. arXiv preprint arXiv:2401.10369 (2024)
19. Lovecruft, I., et al.: Dalek elliptic curve cryptography. Github (2024). https://github.com/dalek-cryptography/curve25519-dalek
20. Kapritsos, M., et al.: All about eve: execute-verify replication for multi-core servers. In: 10th USENIX Symposium on Operating Systems Design and Implementation (OSDI 12), pp. 237–250 (2012)
21. Kotla, R., Alvisi, L., Dahlin, M., Clement, A., Wong, E.: Zyzzyva: speculative byzantine fault tolerance. ACM Trans. Comput. Syst. (TOCS) **27**(4), 1–39 (2010)
22. Lianza, T., Snook, C.: A Byzantine failure in the real world (2020). https://blog.cloudflare.com/a-byzantine-failure-in-the-real-world/
23. Mellanox: Mellanox Innova™ IPsec (2018). https://network.nvidia.com/related-docs/whitepapers/WP_Innova_IPsec.pdf
24. Messadi, I., Kapitza, R.: Cloud-aware bft proactive recovery using confidential computing (2024)
25. Nvidia: ConnectX-6 DX (2021). https://www.nvidia.com/content/dam/en-zz/Solutions/networking/ethernet-adapters/connectX-6-dx-datasheet.pdf
26. Patel, D., Nishball, D., Eliahou Ontiveros, J.: Multi-datacenter training: Openai's ambitious plan to beat google's infrastructure (2024). https://www.semianalysis.com/p/multi-datacenter-training-openais
27. Sousa, P.: Proactive resilience. In: Sixth European Dependable Computing Conference (EDCC-6) Supplemental Volume, pp. 27–32 (2006)
28. Tang, S., et al.: Improved pbft algorithm for high-frequency trading scenarios of alliance blockchain. Sci. Rep. **12**(1), 4426 (2022)
29. Wu, B., et al.: Transom: an efficient fault-tolerant system for training llms. arXiv (2023)

30. Yin, M., et al.: HotStuff: BFT consensus with linearity and responsiveness. In: Proceedings of the ACM Symposium on Principles of Distributed Computing (2019)
31. Zhang, H.: Byzantine fault tolerance in the age of blockchains and cloud computing. In: Proceedings of the Cloud Computing Security Workshop, CCSW'22, p. 5 (2022). https://doi.org/10.1145/3560810.3565288

BCProf: Battery Consumption Profiler for Android Applications

Lyla Naghipour Vijouyeh[1]({{ICON}}), Luís Veiga[2]({{ICON}}), and Paulo Ferreira[1]({{ICON}})

[1] University of Oslo, Oslo, Norway
{lylan,paulofe}@ifi.uio.no
[2] INESC-ID/Técnico Lisboa, ULisboa, Lisbon, Portugal
luis.veiga@inesc-id.pt

Abstract. The widespread use of mobile applications in daily life has raised significant concerns about their energy consumption, as it directly affects user satisfaction, their hosting device longevity, and environmental sustainability. Despite the need for energy-aware mobile application development, developers lack cost-effective, software-based, and intuitive tools to measure and analyze energy usage during the development process. This paper introduces BCProf (Battery Consumption Profiler), a novel framework designed to measure the energy consumption of Android applications at both method and application granularities. BCProf supports both Java and Kotlin languages and is implemented as a plugin for seamless integration into Android Studio.

BCProf works by instrumenting the application's source code with custom log statements that enable tracking Android API calls. During application testing, BCProf monitors the generated logs alongside hardware component usage (e.g., WiFi, GPS, camera, Bluetooth, and screen) to calculate energy consumption. By leveraging this monitored data, BCProf correlates the energy usage of Android API calls and hardware components with specific methods in the application's source code. The tool supports both online, real-time energy analysis during application execution and offline analysis by saving energy usage data in a JSON file format.

Extensive evaluations were conducted across various Android applications to validate the accuracy and versatility of BCProf. The results show that BCProf can achieve up to 98% accuracy under specific conditions. This makes it a reliable and adaptable solution for the energy profiling of Android mobile applications.

Keywords: Energy Consumption · Battery Consumption · Android Application · Plugin · Android Studio · Software

1 Introduction

The global mobile application market is expanding rapidly [31]. This growth is driven by increasing smartphone adoption, enhanced network connectivity, and integration of artificial intelligence and machine learning in mobile applications [34,35]. However, as mobile applications incorporate more complex features, their energy consumption rises, which leads to concerns over battery life, user experience, and sustainability issues. Rapid battery depletion, in particular, negatively affects application ratings and retention [5,30]. As a result, optimizing energy consumption of Android applications has become one of key concerns for developers [19]. To tackle this challenge effectively, developers need first to identify their application's energy consumption patterns and pinpoint the key energy bottlenecks.

There are various tools and techniques available for estimating the energy consumption of Android applications, ranging from those that rely on specialized Hardware (HW) equipment to Software (SW)-based solutions. While SW-based tools are generally more preferred by developers due to their cost-effectiveness and scalability, they also come with several limitations. First, most SW-based tools focus exclusively on either HW or SW components when estimating energy consumption. This narrow focus limits their ability to provide a comprehensive understanding of energy usage in the application, as they fail to account for the combined impact of both HW and SW components. Second, the majority of these tools lack support for Kotlin, despite its growing popularity as the preferred language for Android application development. These limitations restricts their applicability in modern development environments. Additionally, most tools provide only post-execution energy estimation, which offers limited insights compared to real-time energy analysis.

To address these gaps, we propose BCProf (Battery Consumption Profiler),[1] a novel SW-based framework for estimating the energy consumption of Android applications in real time. BCProf estimates energy consumption at both the application and method/function levels by considering both HW components and Android API calls (SW components). To achieve this, BCProf instruments the application's source code with a set of specific log statements, enabling the tracking of Android API calls and HW usage at the method level during execution. While the application runs, BCProf monitors these logs alongside HW components usage to calculate energy consumption. In addition to real-time energy analysis, BCProf supports post-execution energy analysis by saving the results in a JSON [6] file format.

BCProf is implemented as a plugin for Android Studio that enables developers to evaluate energy consumption during the development process. BCProf supports both Kotlin and Java, which makes it a versatile tool suitable for a wide range of projects, from legacy applications developed in Java to modern applications built with Kotlin. Unlike existing tools, BCProf takes into account device-specific and battery-related characteristics, such as battery health and capacity, in estimating energy consumption. It also offers user customization by allowing developers to input these values manually. However, it functions effectively even without such inputs from user by using default values. Additionally, BCProf sup-

---

[1] https://github.com/LylaNV/BCProf.

ports both Android emulators [12] and physical devices as test environments for energy estimation, further enhancing its flexibility.

The key contributions of this paper are as follows:

- Introducing a novel mathematical model for energy consumption of Android applications by considering both HW components and Android API calls, offering a comprehensive approach to energy profiling at the application and method/function levels;
- Integrating battery characteristics (health and capacity) and HW component power values into the mathematical model to provide customizablity and better battery consumption estimations;
- Introducing a software-based tool (BCProf) that enables energy measurements on both Android emulators and physical devices, eliminating the reliance on physical devices for energy testing;
- Implementing the tool as a plugin for Android Studio for seamless integration into development environments, enabling energy measurements in development process;
- Supporting both Java and Kotlin languages, ensuring compatibility with a wide range of projects;
- Performing a comprehensive evaluation to verify the accuracy of BCProf, while demonstrating its practicality and effectiveness in real-world scenarios.

The paper is structured as follows. Section 2 reviews the strengths and limitations of existing tools and outlines research gaps. Section 3 introduces the architecture of BCProf and its constituent modules. The battery consumption model and detail of implementation are described in Sects. 4 and 5, respectively. Section 6 presents evaluation results to validate BCProf's accuracy. Finally, Sect. 7 summarizes the findings and provides concluding insights.

2 Related Work

Energy profiling of Android applications is a complex challenge that has been addressed through various approaches. Tools range from device-wide [7] to application-specific profilers [11,28], each employing different techniques to estimate energy consumption. While some offer broad measurements, others focus on fine-grained insights at the method level [1,3,29,36]. However, they still face limitations, including hardware dependency, scalability issues, and difficulty in accurately attributing energy usage to specific code segments [7,11,28]. This section examines state-of-the-art energy profiling tools, discusses their methodologies, strengths, and limitations, and identifies existing research gaps. Tools requiring specialized HW [18,32] or relying on command-line logs from physical devices [2] are excluded, as they fall beyond the scope of this paper.

PCE [28] is an Android Studio plugin designed to estimate the power consumption of Android applications. They define power automatons for different HW components, such as WiFi, audio, and GPS, which are then optimized based on the application's source code. These optimized automatons are combined to form a comprehensive power automaton that integrates HW power states and their duration to estimate energy consumption for specific test scenarios. Although their tool integrates with Android Studio, it considers only HW components in energy calculations and lacks real-time analysis. Moreover, it estimates energy at the application level and fails to identify the most energy-intensive code segments.

Navitas [29] is an open-source framework for energy profiling of Android applications, particularly those with multi-threading. Implemented as an Android Studio plugin, it instruments application code to log execution traces and thread-specific details. During execution on a physical device, it collects HW component data, such as CPU frequency and screen brightness, to compute method-level energy consumption in Joules. However, it supports only applications developed in Java and does not account for the energy usage of Android API calls.

Orka [36] estimates method-level energy consumption in Android applications through two modules: Injector and Analyzer. The Injector extracts application details and inserts logging methods after Android API calls, while the Analyzer runs the instrumented app on an emulator to collect execution traces and estimate energy usage. Orka is developed in Python for Linux as a web application, though it is not publicly available. Cornet and Gopalan [3] extended Orka to include WiFi energy consumption but did not account for other HW components.

GreenAdvisor [1] is a Java-based tool that predicts energy consumption changes in Android applications by analyzing modifications in system calls usage. It assumes that changes in application system calls can impact energy consumption. The tool monitors these calls using jUnit tests and employs a bag-of-words model to map them to Java methods and identify potential causes of energy variations. It provides reports detailing modified system calls and related code changes. However, GreenAdvisor does not measure energy consumption or determine whether usage has increased or decreased.

Batterystats [11] is an Android framework tool that collects battery usage data from physical devices. This data can be transferred to a development machine via Android Debug Bridge (adb) [8] and visualized using Battery Historian, which generates HTML-based reports. These reports offer insights into battery consumption at both the system and application levels. However, Battery Historian is no longer actively maintained by the Android team. Additionally, it requires a physical Android device, limiting its usability with an emulator. It also fails to identify energy-intensive code segments, as it provides energy estimation only at the application level and device-wide.

The Android Studio Power Profiler [7] visualizes power consumption data collected from the On-Device Power Rails Monitor (ODPM), which categorizes power usage into subsystems like CPU, Camera, Display, and GPS. It leverages the System Trace feature to capture detailed power metrics and relate power usage with application activities. However, the tool operates at the device

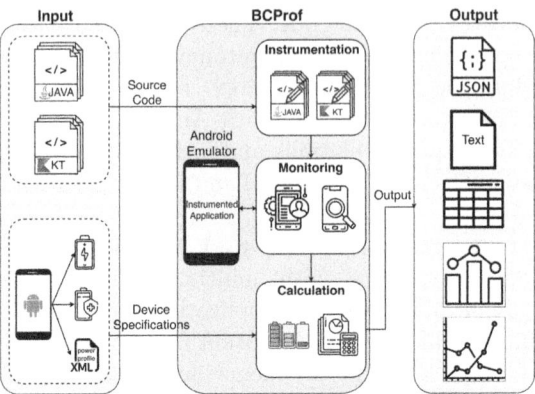

Fig. 1. The high-level overview of BCProf.

level and may include noise from other applications, making it less precise for application-specific analysis. Additionally, ODPM is only supported on Pixel 6 and newer devices running Android 10 (API level 29) or higher, limiting its broader applicability.

The reviewed tools focus solely on either HW or SW components, neglecting the combined contributions of both to energy consumption. Although Cornet and Gopalan [3] considers WiFi usage in addition to Android API calls, it still overlooks other HW components such as GPS, screen, etc. Furthermore, the tools typically provide post-execution energy analysis instead of real-time feedback, which limits their ability to monitor energy consumption while the application is running. Additionally, most tools rely on physical devices, which presents scalability issues as testing on various devices is impractical. Moreover, with the exception of Batterystats and Power Profiler, all the mentioned tools support only Java, while Kotlin is increasingly preferred for Android development. Since Batterystats and Power Profiler do not analyze SW components energy usage (such ad Android API calls), their functionalities remain unaffected by the programming language. Therefore, Kotlin support is irrelevant for these tools. Additionally, existing tools lack user customization for energy model parameters. This limits adaptability for specific devices or needs.

These gaps emphasize the need for a flexible tool that addresses the current limitations. Such a tool should integrate both HW and SW components impact for energy consumption calculation, offer both application-level and method-level analysis, support real-time and offline energy analysis, and be compatible with Android emulators and physical devices. Furthermore, it should allow users to customize test scenarios and parameters. BCProf meets these criteria, seamlessly integrating with Android Studio to help developers optimize their applications' energy usage during development.

3 BCProf Architecture

BCProf is a software-based battery consumption profiler that provides insights into the energy usage of Android applications at both the method/function and application granularities. It helps users (i.e., developers) to identify energy bottlenecks early in the development process without needing a physical Android device. To ensure seamless integration with the development environment, BCProf is developed as a plugin for Android Studio [9,16]. Hereafter, the term method will be used to refer to both methods in Java and functions in Kotlin.

A high-level overview of BCProf is shown in Fig. 1. The framework takes the application's source code as input and instruments it with specific log statements (the instrumentation step in Fig. 1). Then, while the instrumented application runs on an Android emulator [12], it monitors HW components usage and Android API calls (the monitoring step in Fig. 1). Using this data, BCProf calculates the application's battery consumption, as well as the energy usage of individual methods, in real-time. In addition to real-time analysis, it generates a JSON [6] file containing the battery consumption results for offline evaluation.

Figure 2 presents a detailed illustration of BCProf's architecture, which consists of five interconnected modules. These modules work together to instrument the source code, monitor HW components' activity and Android API calls, compute battery consumption, and visualize energy usage data. This section discusses BCProf's inputs, the functionalities of its modules, and the outputs it generates.

3.1 Input

As shown in Fig. 1, BCProf takes two categories of inputs: application source code and device specifications. The source code refers to the source code of the target Android application, corresponding to the open project in Android Studio. BCProf supports all projects developed in Java, Kotlin, or a combination of both.

The device specification category includes the power profile (power_profile.xml), Battery Capacity (BC), and Battery State of Health (SoH). These inputs are optional, and if they are absent, BCProf uses default values. The power profile file contains power usage values (in amperes) for the HW components of a physical Android device. According to the official Android website, device manufacturers must provide this file and embed it within their devices [15]. This file can be retrieved from a physical device using the adb tool [8]. If users do not provide this file, BCProf uses Android estimated power profile values as the default. Battery Capacity (BC) refers to the maximum electrical charge a battery can store when new, expressed in milliampere-hours (mAh) or ampere-hours (Ah). Battery State of Health (SoH) represents the current performance of a battery and is defined as the ratio of its current available capacity to its maximum capacity [37,38]. The default values for BC and SoH are 5000 mAh and 100%, respectively.

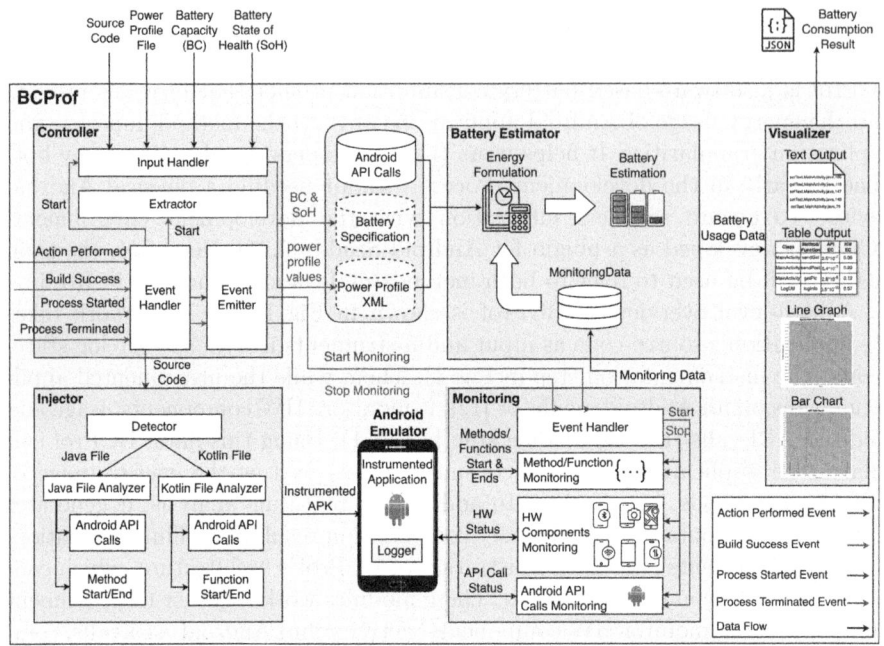

Fig. 2. The architecture of BCProf. (Color figure online)

3.2 Constituent Modules

BCProf consists of five interconnected modules: Controller, Injector, Monitoring, Battery Estimator, and Visualizer modules (see Fig. 2). It also maintains three databases: one for Android API calls energy cost, another for battery specifications (BC and SoH), and a third for power profile of HW components (i.e., power_profile.xml). This section first details each module and its functionalities, then explains the BCProf workflow.

Controller. The main responsibility of the Controller module is to manage other modules. The Controller module is initiated by adding BCProf to Android Studio as a plugin and takes appropriate actions based on the received events through its Event Handler submodule. There are four types of events that the Controller module receives: Action Performed, Build Success, Process Started, and Process Terminated.

Action Performed is triggered when the user starts working with BCProf by clicking on BCProf in Android Studio's Run menu. Upon receiving this event, the Event Handler submodule activates the Input Handler submodule to capture user input. The Input Handler submodule processes the inputs and makes them available to other modules. Additionally, if the user provides a power profile file, BC, or SoH, the Input Handler submodule updates the corresponding databases (blue lines in Fig. 2). Build Success occurs whenever the user successfully builds the project (orange lines in Fig. 2). Upon receiving this event, the Event Handler submodule starts the Extractor submodule, which retrieves application details such as the package name and project path.

Process Started is triggered when the target application runs on an Android emulator. When received, the Event Handler submodule forwards it to the Event Emitter submodule. The Event Emitter submodule then generates a Start Monitoring event to signal the Monitoring module to begin monitoring (green lines in Fig. 2). Process Terminated is triggered when the application's execution stops. Upon receiving this event, the Event Handler submodule sends it to the Event Emitter submodule, which generates a Stop Monitoring event and transmits it to the Monitoring module to halt monitoring (red lines in Fig. 2).

Injector. The injector module is responsible for instrumenting the source code of the target application with BCProf-specific log statements. These log statements enable the Monitoring module to detect the occurrence of Android API calls and the start and end of the method when the target application is running on an Android emulator. The injector module inserts three types of log statements into the source code: methods start, all paths where methods end or exit including early returns and exception handlers, and Android API calls.

The internal structure of the Injector module is shown in Fig. 2. It consists of three main submodules: Detector, Java File Analyzer, and Kotlin File Analyzer. The Detector submodule identifies the type of each source code file (Java or Kotlin) and forwards it to the corresponding Analyzer submodule. The reason for having separate submodules for handling log statements is due to the differences in syntax between Java and Kotlin, as well as the distinct representations of these languages in Android Studio through their Program Structure Interface (PSI).

Monitoring. As illustrated in Fig. 2, the Monitoring module comprises four submodules: Event Handler, Method/Function Monitoring, HW Components Monitoring, and Android API Calls Monitoring. The Event Handler submodule processes two types of events (Start Monitoring and Stop Monitoring) and, depending on the event type, activates or deactivates the relevant submodules.

The Methods/Functions Monitoring and Android API Calls Monitoring submodules analyze system logs retrieved from Android Emulator via the Logcat tool [10]. When a Method Start log appears, the Methods/Functions Monitoring submodule records details about the method, including its timestamp and the current status of HW components. Upon detecting a Method End log, it calculates the execution time and updates the HW component status before sending this information to the Battery Estimator module for further analysis. Similarly, the Android API Calls Monitoring submodule identifies log entries related to Android API calls and transmits them to the Battery Estimator.

The HW Component Monitoring submodule tracks the status of HW components and detects when the application utilizes them. Once HW activity is identified, it sends this data to the Battery Estimator module, which then calculates the battery consumption attributed to the HW components.

Battery Estimator. The Battery Estimator module calculates energy consumption in real-time (while the application is running) at both the application and method levels. It estimates battery usage by considering two primary sources: SW, which refers to Android API calls, and HW, which encompasses the HW components utilized by the application.

To perform these calculations, the module retrieves Android API call data and HW component usage from the Monitoring module, along with their corresponding energy costs from BCProf internal databases. By integrating energy costs from both SW and HW, the Battery Estimator provides a more precise estimation of energy consumption. The energy model used for this estimation is detailed in Sect. 4.

Visualizer. The Visualizer module obtains battery usage data from Battery Estimator (see Fig. 2) and presents the energy consumption results to the user in four formats within Android Studio: Text View, Table View, Bar Graph, and Line Graph.

The Text View presents detailed information about Android API calls, including their locations in the source code, the methods that invoked them, and the classes from which they were accessed. By analyzing this data alongside other outputs, developers can identify specific lines of code contributing to high battery consumption. The Table View provides a breakdown of battery consumption at the method level, distinguishing energy usage attributed to HW components and Android API calls. This helps developers gain insights into the primary sources of battery drain. The Bar Graph View represents Android API calls and their invocation frequency during the application's execution. This helps developers identify the most frequently used APIs. The Line Graph View illustrates the total battery consumption of the application throughout its lifecycle. All views update in real-time while the application runs, which allows developers to receive immediate feedback on battery consumption. When the application stops, the Visualizer module automatically saves the generated outputs in a JSON file [6] to support offline analysis.

BCProf Workflow. The BCProf workflow begins with a user action (starting BCProf). Upon detecting this action, the Controller module prompts the user for optional inputs, such as power profile values, BC, and SoH. If the user provides these inputs, the Controller module updates the corresponding databases. Next, the Controller module initiates the Injector module to instrument the source code. The Injector module inserts BCProf-specific log statements into the target application's source code to enable energy-related data tracking.

When the application is executed the Controller module activates the Monitoring module. This module continuously tracks Android API calls and HW component usage while the application runs on the Android Emulator. The Monitoring module then forwards the collected data to the Battery Estimator module. This module utilizes the monitoring data along with the energy costs of API calls and HW components, which it retrieves from the databases, to calculate real-time energy consumption. The computed battery usage data is subsequently sent to the Visualizer module, which presents the results to the user.

When the application stops, the Controller module triggers a Stop Monitoring event. Upon receiving this event, the Monitoring module ceases tracking API calls and HW usage on the Android Emulator.

4 Battery Consumption Model

BCProf accounts for two primary sources of energy usage in Android applications: (1) HW components and (2) Android API calls. In this section, we first explain the energy consumption model of HW components and Android API calls. Then, we present the formulation for total battery consumption by integrating these energy contributions into a comprehensive formula. All the notations used in this section are listed in Table 1.

Table 1. Notations: Parameters and Variables

Symbol	Description
BC	Battery capacity measured in mAh
SoH	State of Health of the battery, presented as a percentage
T	Set of battery update timings
HW	Set of all hardware components
API	Set of all Android API calls
$Method$	Set of all methods in the application's code
b_a	Battery usage from API call a
$I_h^{t_i}$	Current of hardware component h at time t_i in mA
$BU(API)^{t_i}$	Battery usage of all Android API calls at time t_i
$BU(HW)^{t_i}$	Battery usage of all hardware components at time t_i
$BU_h^{t_i}$	Battery usage of hardware component h at time t_i
$bl_{screen}^{t_i} \in [1-255]$	Screen brightness level at time t_i
$x_{m,a}^{t_i} \in \{0,1\}$	Equals 1 if method m invokes API call a at time t_i
$y_h^{t_i} \in \{0,1\}$	Equals 1 if hardware component h is active at time t_i

Hardware Components Energy Model. The battery usage of HW component h at time t_i is modeled using Eq. 1.

$$BU_h^{t_i} = y_h^{t_i} \times \frac{\Delta t_i \times I_h^{t_i}}{SoH \times BC \times 3600} \times 100 \qquad (1)$$

The variable $y_h^{t_i}$ specifies whether the hardware component h is active at time t_i. The parameter $I_h^{t_i}$ represents the current drawn by the HW component h. SoH and BC denote the battery state of health and capacity, respectively. The constant value of 3600 is included in the formula to maintain unit consistency by converting mAs to mAh, the standard unit for battery capacity. We assume that battery estimation updates occur at one-second intervals. The ith instance of battery usage calculation is denoted by t_i. Thus, the difference between two consecutive battery updates is given by $\Delta t_i = t_i - t_{i-1} = 1$ second. However, this interval can be adjusted.

The impact of SoH is incorporated into the formulation as it greatly affects the battery's effective capacity [4]. By accounting for this factor, our approach enhances calculation accuracy compared to methods that consider only BC. This ensures that the effects of battery aging (SoH) are properly reflected in battery consumption estimates. To establish the relationship between BC and SoH, we follow a methodology aligned with well-established studies [33,37,38], adhering to best practices in the field.

The parameter $I_h^{t_i}$ is derived from power profile values and represents the power drawn by the HW component h. BCProf supports HW components such as camera, GPS, WiFi, radio, Bluetooth, and screen. For most of these components $I_h^{t_i}$ remains the constant over time (i.e., $I_h^{t_0} = I_h^{t_1} = I_h^{t_2} = \ldots = I_h^{t_i} = \ldots = I_h^{t_{|T|}}$). However, the screen current varies depending on the brightness level which is calculated using Eq. 2 with brightness level $bl_{screen}^{t_i}$ ranging from 1 to 255 [17].

$$I_{screen}^{t_i} = I_{screen\_on} + \left(\frac{I_{screen\_full} \times bl_{screen}^{t_i}}{255} \right) \qquad (2)$$

For the remaining HW components, the power consumption values are specified as $I_{wifi} = I_{wifi\_active}$, $I_{camera} = I_{camera\_avg}$, $I_{radio} = I_{radio\_active}$, $I_{gps} = I_{gps\_on}$, and $I_{bluetooth} = I_{bluetooth\_active}$.

The total battery usage of HW components at t_i is calculated using Eq. 3, which represents the sum of the battery usage of all active HW components at t_i.

$$BU(HW)^{t_i} = \sum_{h \in HW} BU_h^{t_i} \qquad (3)$$

API Calls Energy Model. The battery usage associated with Android API calls at time t_i is determined as the sum of the battery consumption of all Android API calls invoked by methods since t_{i-1}. This is modeled by Eq. 4.

$$BU(API)^{t_i} = \sum_{m \in Methods} \sum_{a \in API} x_{m,a}^{t_i} \times b_a \qquad (4)$$

The variable $x_{m,a}^{t_i}$ determines whether method m has invoked API call a during the interval from t_{i-1} to t_i, while b_a represents the energy cost (i.e., battery use) of API call a. To quantify the energy cost of Android API calls, we conducted benchmarking and measured their battery consumption.

Total Energy Consumption Model. As previously mentioned, BCProf accounts for the energy consumption of both HW components and Android API calls into account. Given the models we have presented for HW components and API calls, the application's battery usage at t_i can be determined using Eq. 5.

$$BU(total)^{t_i} = BU(API)^{t_i} + BU(HW)^{t_i} \tag{5}$$

The total battery consumption of the application from the time it starts running up to the current time can be computed using Eq. 6.

$$BU(total) = \left(\sum_{t_i \in T} BU(HW)^{t_i}\right) + \left(\sum_{t_i \in T} BU(API)^{t_i}\right) \tag{6}$$

The Battery Estimator in BCProf utilizes Eq. 6 to estimate the battery consumption of Android applications. This formula incorporates the energy impact of both API calls and HW components.

5 Implementation

BCProf is implemented in Java as an Android Studio plugin based on IntelliJ Platform [26]. This ensures seamless integration into the Android Studio environment and enables energy analysis during the development process. BCProf is platform-independent and runs on any operating system supported by Android Studio, including Windows, macOS, and Linux [9].

In implementing BCProf, three key IntelliJ Platform concepts are leveraged: Actions [20], Listeners [23], and Extensions [24]. Actions are used to implement the core functionalities of the Controller module and enable user interaction with BCProf. BCProf subscribes to the Android Build Listener [22] to identify whether the application has been successfully built. Additionally, it subscribes to the IntelliJ Execution Listener [25] to detect application start (Process Started) and stop (Process Terminated) events, subsequently activating or halting the Monitoring and Battery Estimator modules.

BCProf extends the IntelliJ Platform ToolWindow [27] framework to provide an intuitive and accessible interface for result analysis. To support multiple output formats including text, tables, bar charts, and line graphs, we utilize the JFreeChart library.[2] The ToolWindow updates in real-time to provide dynamic feedback to developers as the target application runs on an Android emulator. Additionally, BCProf saves the output in a JSON file to enable developers to revisit and analyze energy consumption results at any time.

As mentioned in Sect. 3, BCProf instruments the application with specific log statements through its Injector module. To accomplish this, BCProf analyzes the source code, identifies relevant lines, and inserts log statements at the appropriate locations. BCProf leverages Program Structure Interface (PSI) in the IntelliJ Framework for this purpose. In the IntelliJ Framework, a PSI file

---
[2] https://github.com/jfree/jfreechart.

serves as the root of a hierarchical structure that represents a file's contents as language-specific elements [21]. Since BCProf supports both Java and Kotlin, it employs both PsiJavaFile and KtFile.

6 Evaluation

In this section, we evaluate BCProf's accuracy and practicality in estimating energy consumption. We begin by outlining the evaluation setup and then follow with a detailed analysis of the results.

To evaluate BCProf, we assess its performance across four scenarios. Scenario 1 examines BCProf's accuracy in estimating an application's overall energy consumption by considering both HW components and Android API calls energy usage. This scenario specifically targets GPS, WiFi, and Camera to demonstrate BCProf's ability to capture their impact. Scenario 2 evaluates the effect of SoH on energy estimation and verifies that BCProf accounts for this factor. Scenario 3 tests BCProf's capability to estimate energy consumption regardless of the programming language. To do so, we compare the energy usage of an application developed in both Java and Kotlin. Scenario 4 explores the influence of screen brightness by measuring energy consumption at different brightness levels to validate BCProf's sensitivity to these variations.

Evaluation Setup. We developed four test applications to evaluate BCProf: Camera, Video, Client, and GPS. The Camera application captures and displays a picture, while the Video application plays a user-selected video, targeting the camera and screen, respectively. The Client application, designed for WiFi evaluation, performs server availability checks, user data submissions, and image retrieval without caching. A locally hosted Python server handles its requests. The GPS application retrieves the user's location, ensuring fresh data by enforcing high-accuracy settings. To automate the testing process, we employed Espresso [14] and UI Automator [13] to create test scripts for each application.

To evaluate the proposed framework, we compare BCProf's results with those obtained from a physical device. Additionally, we customize BCProf by inputting power profile values derived from the same physical device used for evaluation.

Table 2. Evaluation Settings

Android API Calls Energy Cost				HW Components Power		
Android API Call	Energy Cost	Android API Call	Energy Cost	Component	BCProf default (mA)	Tuned BCProf (mA)
onCreate	$3.9 * 10^{-4}$	Log.e	$1.76 * 10^{-10}$	screen.on	200	120
performClick	$3.49246 * 10^{-9}$	startActivityForResult	$4.3137 * 10^{-4}$	screen.full	200	311
getStringExtra	$1.39699 * 10^{-10}$	findViewById	$2.56114 * 10^{-11}$	wifi.active	31	140
getIntExtra	$1.67638 * 10^{-10}$	setContentView	$1.6 * 10^{-5}$	radio.active	200	200
putExtra	$1.47536 * 10^{-10}$	setText	$3.49246 * 10^{-9}$	camera.avg	600	550
Log.i	$1.76 * 10^{-10}$	getText	$3.4874 * 10^{-9}$	bluetooth.active	20	20
Log.d	$1.76 * 10^{-10}$	finish	$3.879 * 10^{-4}$	gps.on	50	31

This customized version is referred to as Tuned BCProf. This customization demonstrates BCProf's adaptability and improves accuracy by aligning emulator and physical device conditions. Furthermore, we assess BCProf against HW-only and SW-only approaches, where the former considers only HW energy consumption and the latter focuses solely on Android API calls.

The physical Android device used in all scenarios is a Motorola Moto G24 smartphone with a 5000 mAh battery running Android 14. Evaluations of all other approaches were conducted on a MacBook Pro (64 GB RAM, macOS Sequoia 15.3) using Android Studio Ladybug with the BCProf plugin enabled. To ensure consistency and minimize noise, a custom Android Virtual Device (AVD) was configured to match the Motorola Moto G24's specifications, including screen size, OS, RAM, and storage.

As mentioned before, BCProf calculates energy consumption by considering battery SoH, BC, power profile values, and energy usage of Android APIs. In all scenarios, SoH and BC are set to 100% and 5000 mAh, except in Scenario 2, where the impact of SoH is analyzed, and SoH is set to 97%. This value was obtained by averaging the results from two applications, AccuBattery[3] and Battery One[4], which measured the physical device's battery SoH as 95% and 99%, respectively. For Tuned BCProf, power values were fetched from the Motorola Moto G24 device using the adb tool, whereas the default BCProf relies on power data from Android documentation. The energy cost of Android API calls is determined through extensive benchmarking, where API calls were executed in large loops, and battery level changes were recorded to calculate their energy consumption. Table 2 presents the benchmark results for commonly used APIs alongside power values for hardware components.

Since the relationship between user-visible brightness (0–100%) and actual brightness levels (1–255) is non-linear, we conducted an experiment on the Moto G24 to determine their correlation. The brightness levels are then adjusted based on this correlation in the evaluations.

Evaluation Results. This section outlines the evaluation results. To ensure consistency and minimize noise, we generated random strings and numbers that were used uniformly across all scenarios and test runs. In this section, BL represents brightness level.

---

[3] https://play.google.com/store/apps/details?id=com.digibites.accubattery.
[4] https://play.google.com/store/apps/details?id=com.oneapps.batteryone.

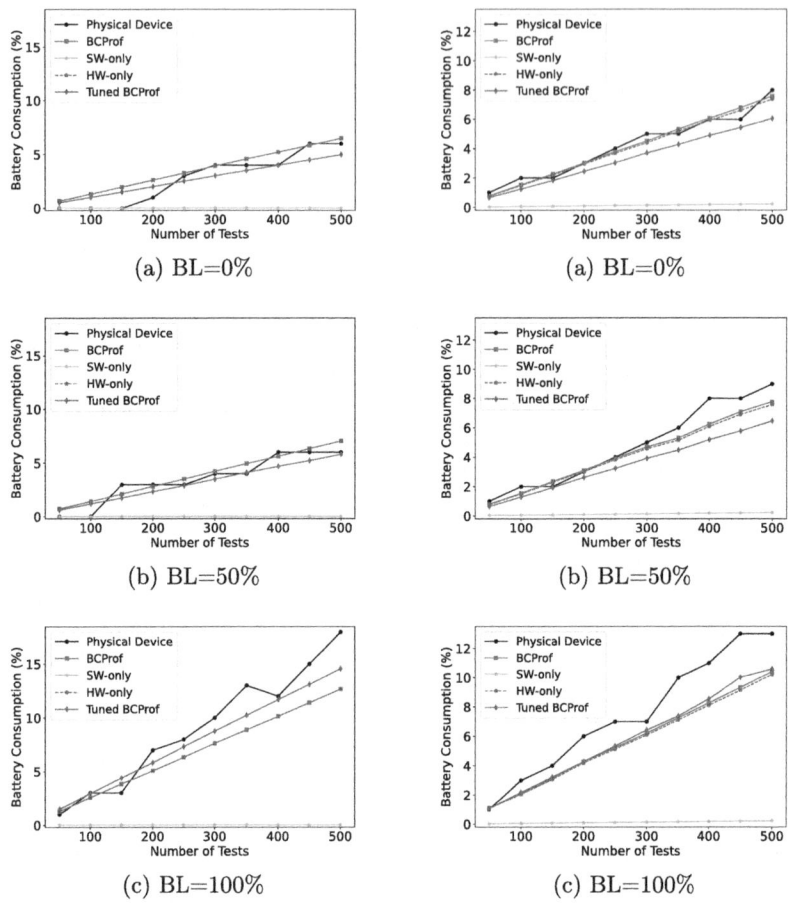

Fig. 3. Client battery consumption. **Fig. 4.** Camera battery consumption.

Figures 3 to 5 present the results for Scenario 1 while increasing the number of tests at three different brightness levels. As shown in Figs. 3a to 3c, at all brightness levels, the Tuned BCProf, BCProf, and HW-only approaches provide competitive energy estimations, while the SW-only approach fails to accurately reflect the application's energy consumption. However, as illustrated in Fig. 3c, Tuned BCProf achieves 81% accuracy at brightness level 100% for the Client application, outperforming both HW-only and BCProf by reducing the error rate by 36%. It is worth noting that the energy estimation by SW-only increases as the number of loops increases; however, due to the scale of the figures, it appears flat. The poor performance of the SW-only approach is due to the limited number of Android API calls in the test applications. In real-world applications, the contribution of SW-only is higher due to greater complexity and increased use of Android API calls.

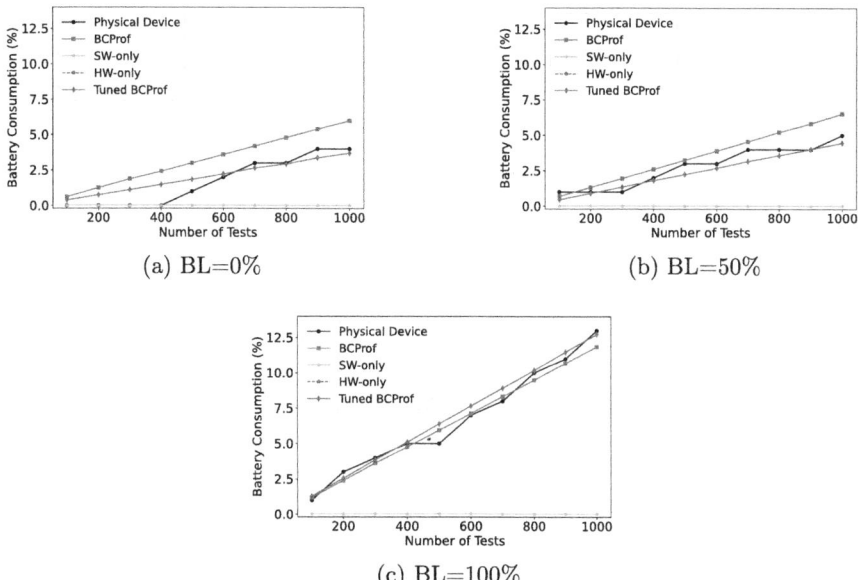

Fig. 5. GPS battery consumption.

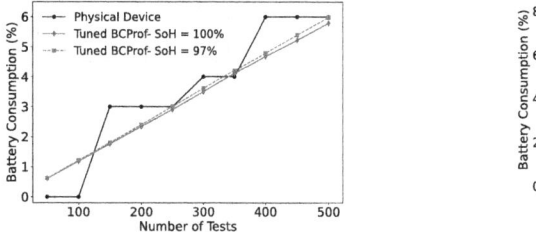

Fig. 6. Impact of SoH.

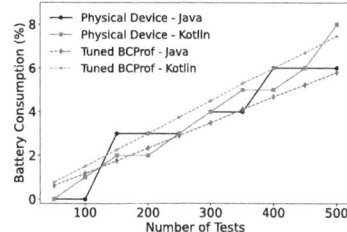

Fig. 7. Kotlin vs Java.

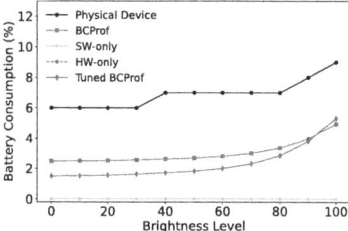

Fig. 8. BL impact.

Figures 4a to 4c present the results for the Camera application. As shown, BCProf outperforms other methods at brightness levels of 0% and 50% due to the higher considered power profile value for the camera (see Table 2). Although BCProf and HW-only approaches provide better energy estimation in some cases (Fig. 4a and Fig. 4b) due to the high camera power value, Tuned BCProf produces more realistic results. The reason is that in this test case, the physical device switches from the application to the native camera app in the device to capture a picture, which causes a spike in CPU and memory usage, and consequently, higher energy consumption. This switching overhead is not considered in our energy model, which explains the poorer performance of Tuned BCProf compared to BCProf and HW-only approaches.

Figures 5a to 5c demonstrate the battery consumption results for the GPS application. As shown, Tuned BCProf outperforms all the other approaches by accuracy rates 92.4%, 89%, and 98% at BLs of 0%, 50%, and 100%, respectively.

Figure 6 illustrates the impact of SoH on energy estimations for the Client application. It compares the battery consumption of the Client application on the physical device, Tuned BCProf with SoH = 100% and Tuned BCProf with SoH = 97%. As shown in Fig. 6, considering the SoH improves BCProf's energy estimation by reducing the error by approximately 90%.

Figure 7 presents the energy consumption of the Client application at 50% BL, comparing implementations in Java and Kotlin. BCProf effectively captures the energy consumption pattern for both, which demonstrates that BCProf not only supports Java applications but also provides precise estimations for Kotlin.

Figure 8 illustrates the impact of screen brightness (BL) on energy estimation. BL is increased from 0% to 100% in 10% increments, with 50 test iterations per step to measure the Video application's battery consumption. Except for the SW-only approach, all methods provide competitive estimates. Since the test count remains constant, API-related energy remains unchanged across BL variations. While BCProf and HW-only perform well below 60% BL due to higher screen power values (Table 2), they fail to capture actual battery consumption patterns. Tuned BCProf, leveraging the power profile from the physical device, better reflects energy trends and reduces error by 11% compared to BCProf at 100% BL.

7 Conclusion

This paper presents BCProf, a framework for estimating the battery consumption of Android applications at both method and application levels. It is implemented as an Android Studio plugin and empowers developers to measure energy usage during development process without requiring physical devices. By supporting both Java and Kotlin, BCProf ensures usability in wide range of projects.

To estimate the battery consumption of Android applications, BCProf accounts on both Android API calls and HW components energy usages. It instruments the source code with specific log statements to enable monitoring of Android API calls along with monitoring HW usage of methods. Then, while the target application runs, it calculates the energy consumption on real-time and also saves the output for post-execution analysis. BCProf incorporates battery SoH and BC to improve the energy estimation.

Extensive evaluations show that BCProf outperforms existing approaches and can achieve up to 98% accuracy in estimating the energy consumption of Android applications. The results demonstrate its effectiveness in capturing the impact of various HW components and brightness levels on energy consumption. Additionally, the results show that BCProf enhances accuracy by incorporating SoH alongside BC in the energy estimation model. As a future work, we plan to extend BCProf by utilizing Large Language Models to offer energy refactoring to the users in addition to energy consumption estimation.

Acknowledgments. The work by Luís Veiga was supported by Fundação para a Ciência e a Tecnologia (FCT), under project UIDB/50021/2020 (DOI: 10.54499/UIDB/50021/2020).

References

1. Aggarwal, K., Hindle, A., Stroulia, E.: GreenAdvisor: a tool for analyzing the impact of software evolution on energy consumption. In: 2015 IEEE International Conference on Software Maintenance and Evolution (ICSME), pp. 311–320. IEEE, IEEE, Bremen, Germany, September 2015
2. Bouaffar, F., Le Goaer, O., Noureddine, A.: PowDroid: energy profiling of android applications. In: 2021 36th IEEE/ACM International Conference on Automated Software Engineering Workshops (ASEW), pp. 251–254. IEEE, November 2021
3. Cornet, A., Gopalan, A.: A software-based approach for source-line level energy estimates and hardware usage accounting on android. In: The Eighth International Conference on Smart Grids. Green Communications and IT Energy-aware Technologies, pp. 32–37. IARIA, Nice, France (2018)
4. Das, K., Kumar, R., Krishna, A.: Analyzing electric vehicle battery health performance using supervised machine learning. Renew. Sustain. Energy Rev. **189**, 113967 (2024)
5. Elliott, J., Kor, A., Omotosho, O.A.: Energy consumption in smartphones: an investigation of battery and energy consumption of media related applications on android smartphones. In: International SEEDS Conference, December 2017
6. Erickson, J.: What is json? (2024). https://www.oracle.com/database/what-is-json/. Accessed Feb 2025
7. Google: Power Profiler|Android Studio (2023). https://developer.android.com/studio/profile/power-profiler. Accessed Feb 2025
8. Google: Android debug bridge (ADB) (2024). https://developer.android.com/tools/adb. Accessed Feb 2025
9. Google: Install android studio (2024). https://developer.android.com/studio/install. Accessed Feb 2025
10. Google: Logcat command-line tool (2024). https://developer.android.com/tools/logcat. Accessed Feb 2025
11. Google: Profile battery usage with Batterystats and Battery Historian | App quality (2024). https://developer.android.com/topic/performance/power/setup-battery-historian. Accessed Feb 2025
12. Google: Run apps on the android emulator (2024). https://developer.android.com/studio/run/emulator. Accessed Feb 2025

13. Google: Write automated tests with ui automator (2024). https://developer.android.com/training/testing/other-components/ui-automator. Accessed Feb 2025
14. Google: Espresso (2025). https://developer.android.com/training/testing/espresso. Accessed Feb 2025
15. Google: Measure power values (2025). https://source.android.com/docs/core/power/values. Accessed Feb 2025
16. Google: Meet android studio (2025). https://developer.android.com/studio/intro. Accessed Feb 2025
17. Google: Settings.system#screen_brightness (2025). https://developer.android.com/reference/android/provider/Settings.System#SCREEN_BRIGHTNESS. Accessed Feb 2025
18. Hindle, A., Wilson, A., Rasmussen, K., Barlow, E.J., Campbell, J.C., Romansky, S.: GreenMiner: a hardware based mining software repositories software energy consumption framework. In: Proceedings of the 11th Working Conference on Mining Software Repositories, pp. 12–21. MSR 2014, Association for Computing Machinery, New York, NY, USA, May 2014
19. Hu, Y., Yan, J., Yan, D., Lu, Q., Yan, J.: Lightweight energy consumption analysis and prediction for Android applications. Sci. Comput. Program. **162**, 132–147 (2018)
20. JetBrains: Actions (2023). https://plugins.jetbrains.com/docs/intellij/plugin-actions.html. Accessed Feb 2025
21. JetBrains: Psi files (2023). https://plugins.jetbrains.com/docs/intellij/psi-files.html. Accessed Feb 2025
22. JetBrains: Android plugin extension point and listener list (2024). https://plugins.jetbrains.com/docs/intellij/android-plugin-extension-point-list.html. Accessed Feb 2025
23. JetBrains: Listeners (2024). https://plugins.jetbrains.com/docs/intellij/plugin-listeners.html. Accessed Feb 2025
24. JetBrains: Extensions (2025). https://plugins.jetbrains.com/docs/intellij/plugin-extensions.html. Accessed Feb 2025
25. JetBrains: Intellij platform extension point and listener list (2025). https://plugins.jetbrains.com/docs/intellij/intellij-platform-extension-point-list.html. Accessed Feb 2025
26. JetBrains: IntelliJ Platform: Open Source Platform for Building IDEs and Developer Tools (2025). https://www.jetbrains.com/opensource/idea/. Accessed Feb 2025
27. JetBrains: Tool windows (2025). https://plugins.jetbrains.com/docs/intellij/tool-windows.html. Accessed Feb 2025
28. Le, H.A., Bui, A.T., Truong, N.T.: An approach to modeling and estimating power consumption of mobile applications. Mobile Netw. App. **24**, 124–133 (2019)
29. Myasnikov, V., Shaposhnikov, A., Sartasov, S., Gordienko, E., Aphonina, O., Gamaonov, A.: Navitas framework: a novel tool for android applications energy profiling. In: 6th Conference on Software Engineering and Information Management (SEIM-2021), p. 11. No. Apr., St. Petersburg, Russia (2021)
30. Park, K., jin Kim, H.: Understanding mobile application usage using battery status and Wi-Fi network. ITS Online Event, 14-17 June 2020, International Telecommunications Society (ITS), June 2020
31. Research, G.V.: Mobile Application Market Size, Share & Growth Report 2030 (2024). https://www.grandviewresearch.com/industry-analysis/mobile-application-market. Accessed Feb 2025

32. Rice, A., Hay, S.: Decomposing power measurements for mobile devices. In: 2010 IEEE International Conference on Pervasive Computing and Communications (PerCom), pp. 70–78. IEEE, IEEE, Mannheim, Germany, March 2010
33. Ungurean, L., Cârstoiu, G., Micea, M.V., Groza, V.: Battery state of health estimation: a structured review of models, methods and commercial devices. Int. J. Energy Res. **41**(2), 151–181 (2017)
34. Vijouyeh, L.N., Bruno, R., Ferreira, P.: EdgeEmu - emulator for android edge devices. In: Patiño-Martínez, M., Paulo, J. (eds.) Distributed Applications and Interoperable Systems. DAIS 2023. LNCS, vol. 13909, pp. 110–127. Springer, Cham (2023). https://doi.org/10.1007/978-3-031-35260-7_7
35. Vijouyeh, L.N., Bruno, R., Ferreira, P.: Emulation tool for android edge devices. In: Proceedings of the 2024 IEEE/ACM 46th International Conference on Software Engineering: Companion Proceedings, pp. 109–113. ICSE-Companion 2024, Association for Computing Machinery, New York, NY, USA (2024)
36. Westfield, B., Gopalan, A.: Orka: a new technique to profile the energy usage of android applications. In: 2016 5th International Conference on Smart Cities and Green ICT Systems (SMARTGREENS), pp. 1–12. No. Apr., IEEE, Rome, Italy (2016)
37. Yang, B., et al.: Critical summary and perspectives on state-of-health of lithium-ion battery. Renew. Sustain. Energy Rev. **190**, 114077 (2024)
38. Zhang, X., Han, Y., Zhang, W.: A review of factors affecting the lifespan of lithium-ion battery and its health estimation methods. Trans. Electr. Electron. Mater. **22**, 567–574 (2021)

GT-LSTM: Integrating High-Resolution Particulate Matter Data for Urban Air Quality Forecasting

Maryam Rahmani[1](✉), Suzanne Crumeyrolle[2], Nadège Martiny[3], and Romain Rouvoy[1]

[1] Univ. Lille, Inria, CNRS, UMR 9189 CRIStAL, Lille, France
maryam.rahmani@inria.fr
[2] Univ. Lille, CNRS, UMR 8518 LOA, Lille, France
[3] Univ. Bourgogne Europe, CNRS, UMR 6282 Biogéosciences, Dijon, France

Abstract. Air pollution remains a critical environmental and public health challenge in urban areas, which requires accurate and efficient predictive models to mitigate its impact. This study introduces a novel spatiotemporal model, *Graph Temporal LSTM* (GT-LSTM), which integrates *Machine Learning* (ML) techniques to forecast air pollution levels, with a focus on Particulate Matter $(PM)_{2.5}$ concentrations. By combining *Graph Convolutional Network* (GCN) to capture spatial dependencies and *Long Short-Term Memory* (LSTM) to model temporal patterns, the proposed framework provides precise and localized predictions in urban and suburban regions.

Our analysis demonstrates the competitive predictive capabilities of the model, achieving high *Coefficient of determination* (R^2) and low error values, highlighting its robustness in correlating predicted and observed pollutant levels. The GT-LSTM model effectively incorporates historical data, neighboring influences, and local pollution sources, allowing reliable short- and long-term forecasts, even in data-short environments.

In addition to its predictive accuracy, the model prioritizes computational efficiency and scalability, using cost-effective sensor networks to expand coverage and reduce the dependence on traditional data sources. By offering fine-grained insights into air quality patterns, this approach supports real-time monitoring, long-term planning, and proactive decision-making, benefiting policymakers and urban residents alike. This study underscores the transformative potential of spatiotemporal modeling and ML techniques in enhancing air pollution monitoring systems, ultimately contributing to improved air quality management and public health outcomes.

Keywords: Graph Neural Networks · Temporal LSTM · Spatiotemporal Forecasting · Air Pollution Prediction · Air Quality Sensor Networks · Particulate Matter Modeling · Air Quality Monitoring · Deep Learning for Environmental Data · Dynamic Graph Learning · Time Series Forecasting

1 Introduction

As global climate change accelerates, its consequences on environmental and public health grow increasingly severe. Among these, air pollution emerges, not only as a contributor to climate change, but also as a critical standalone threat to human health and ecological stability [1,22].

Air pollution encompasses a variety of harmful substances, including *Particulate Matters* (PMs), *Nitrogen Oxides* (NOx), *Sulfur Dioxide* (SO_2), *Ozone* (O_3), and *Volatile Organic Compounds* (VOCs). In particular, PM, consisting of fine particles like $PM_{2.5}$ and PM_{10}, has been strongly linked to respiratory and cardiovascular diseases [15]. Given its dual role in climate dynamics and health outcomes, improving air pollution forecasting is essential for sustainable urban planning, real-time policy interventions, and public well-being.

Identifying the main pollutant sources is crucial for accurate forecasting and for supporting strategic planning in various sectors, from large-scale industries to small-scale agricultural enterprises [11].

This proactive approach enables the implementation of effective measures to mitigate environmental impacts and promote sustainable development [3]. However, the need for accurate, high-resolution air pollution forecasting is particularly pressing in urban areas, where it is essential to address both temporal forecasting and the spatial granularity of forecasting across different site locations within the city, especially for pollutants such as $PM_{2.5}$. Conventional models often rely on data from a limited number of monitoring stations, which may fail to capture the complex dynamics of air pollution in densely populated areas [16].

Air quality forecasting often involves the use of various *Artificial Intelligence* (AI) methods, including *Long Short-Term Memory*s (LSTMs) networks [28], *support vector machines*, and *random forests*, which are applied to multidimensional time series data [25]. These methods, while differing in approach, have been shown to improve the accuracy and efficiency of predictions. However, the effectiveness of each method can vary depending on the dataset and problem context, with LSTMs often performing particularly well in capturing temporal dependencies.

While temporal analysis is important, integrating spatiotemporal considerations into forecasting models is equally critical for a comprehensive understanding of air quality [10]. Traditional approaches, including physical or chemical models, fail to account for the spatial variability of pollutant concentrations across different urban neighborhoods [19]. Air pollution impacts vary significantly between areas due to factors like traffic density, industrial, residential and agriculture activities, and land use patterns. Therefore, a more nuanced approach is needed to provide detailed information on pollutant sources and urban topology [30].

Incorporating spatiotemporal data into air quality forecasting models enables detailed analysis of pollution trends, identification of emission hotspots, and assessment of exposure risks for vulnerable populations. By leveraging data from multiple monitoring stations and employing advanced *Machine Learning* (ML) techniques—particularly graph-based models such as glsplgnn and *Graph Attention Networks* (GATs)—these models can effectively capture complex interactions between local emissions, meteorological factors, and geographic features, thereby improving prediction accuracy [7].

This research presents a spatiotemporal forecasting framework that integrates ML-based graph modeling with air quality data, focusing on the city of Dijon, France. The approach delivers localized forecasts to support targeted interventions and data-driven policy decisions for air quality management [12].

To improve the accuracy of short-term $PM_{2.5}$ forecasting, we introduce a hybrid model that combines *Graph Convolutional Networks* (GCNs) and LSTMs within a temporal attention framework. By incorporating spatial relationships from sensor networks into our previously validated LSTM-based architecture, the model captures local pollution dynamics more effectively-especially in suburban areas with sparse monitoring infrastructure. It enables flexible prediction windows ranging from one hour to over 24 h.

The rest of this paper is organized as follows: Sect. 2 reviews related work, Sects. 3 and 4 describe the methodology and dataset, Sect. 5 presents experimental results, and Sect. 6 concludes with key findings and future research directions.

2 Related Works

Over the past two decades, significant research has focused on forecasting air quality using ML algorithms. The release of pollutants, such as PMs, NOx, SO2, O3, and VOCs, into the atmosphere raises serious risks to human health and ecosystems [23]. Accurate and timely air pollution forecasts are, therefore, crucial for mitigating these adverse effects, making this a major concern for researchers.

Traditional statistical models, such as regression and time series analysis, have been used to predict air pollution levels. However, these methods often struggle to capture the complex, nonlinear relationships inherent in air quality data [29]. To overcome these limitations, ML techniques, including *Support Vector Machines* (SVMs), *Artificial Neural Networks* (ANNs), and *Recurrent Neural Networks*s (RNNs), have been explored [20]. Although these models demonstrate strong capabilities in capturing temporal patterns, they often fail to account for spatial dependencies [14,20].

In particular, Belavadi *et al.* [2] developed a scalable architecture for real-time air quality monitoring and forecasting by integrating wireless sensor networks with government-provided open data. While the system demonstrated strong potential, it also highlighted challenges posed by temporal variability in air quality across regions. To address these challenges, subsequent studies, such as [5], employed LSTM models to capture temporal dynamics and emphasized the role of meteorological factors in enhancing predictive accuracy.

Recognizing the limitations of temporal-only models, researchers have increasingly focused on integrating spatial dependencies through spatiotemporal architectures. Some methods combine *Convolutional Neural Networks* (CNNs) with LSTMs to jointly model spatial and temporal patterns [26]. For example, Gilik *et al.* [9] proposed a CNN-LSTM model to forecast pollutant concentrations across urban locations and enable model transferability between cities. Similarly, Unjin Pak *et al.* [24] applied this approach to predict daily average $PM_{2.5}$ concentrations, though the model's complexity and data dependency may hinder broader applicability.

Zhang Qi *et al.* [31] introduced Deep-AIR, a hybrid CNN-LSTM model that incorporates domain-specific features like street canyon effects to improve city-scale pollution forecasting. While Deep-AIR yields promising results, its reliance on granular urban data may limit its generalizability to finer spatial scales.

Graph-based models have gained popularity for their ability to capture spatial dependencies. GCNs represent monitoring stations as graph nodes, with edges defined by geographic proximity or pollution similarity [4]. Hofman *et al.* [13] demonstrated that combining GCNs with RNNs improves forecasting accuracy by modeling both spatial and temporal structures. Their work also explored mobile sensor data to generate high-resolution air quality maps, outperforming traditional interpolation methods. Despite these advances, such models remain sensitive to data quality, sensor density, and regional variability.

To further address spatiotemporal complexities, Liang *et al.* [8] proposed the *Multi-scale Spatio-Temporal Graph Convolution Network* (MST-GCN), which effectively captures multi-level spatial correlations and long-term temporal dependencies. Although MST-GCN surpasses baseline models and addresses multi-source data challenges, its sophisticated architecture increases computational costs.

A more recent development is the *Spatiotemporal Graph Convolutional Recurrent Neural Network* (Spatiotemporal GCRNN) [17], which integrates GCNs with RNNs in a lightweight architecture. While the Spatiotemporal GCRNN is smaller and more efficient than prior models such as ConvLSTM [18], it still relies heavily on comprehensive and diverse data sources.

To overcome limitations in existing forecasting models-such as their reliance on dense urban datasets or computationally intensive methods-this study emphasizes *computational efficiency* and *scalability*. Leveraging low-cost in-situ sensors, the proposed framework models both spatial and temporal dependencies using a lightweight GCN-LSTM architecture. This design reduces dependence on costly traditional data sources and supports fine-grained, subarea-level forecasting in regions with sparse sensor coverage.

3 Method

The primary objective of this research is to forecast air pollution levels within a specific time frame by using historical environmental data from various areas within a city. Specifically, our focus is on predicting $PM_{2.5}$ pollutant levels for different areas by analyzing characteristics of spatio-temporal datasets in urban regions.

The problem statement is defined using a weighted graph $G = (N, E)$ to represent the topological structure of the city. Each measurement station is treated as a node, where N represents the set of station nodes $N = [N_1, N_2, ..., N_n]$, n is the total number of nodes. The edge set, denoted as E, defines connections between nodes, illustrating how one node is linked to another. We represent this set of edges with a special adjacency matrix. The adjacency matrix A, denoted as $A \in R^{n \times n}$, visually represents the connections between nodes based on the correlation coefficients obtained from the topology of the city.

Pearson's algorithm is employed to compute the correlation coefficient between node pairs, constructing the adjacency matrix A. As shown in Eq. 1, X and Y represent the measurements from two sensor nodes, Cov signifies the covariance, and σ represents the standard deviation. The key advantage of using Pearson correlation lies in its ability to quantify the linear relationship between measurements, capturing how similarly nodes behave over time. Unlike distance-based measures, Pearson correlation can reveal meaningful connections between nodes that may not be geographically close but exhibit similar pollution patterns due to shared environmental factors. This approach enhances the model's ability to capture complex spatial dependencies beyond mere spatial proximity.

$$P_{X,Y} = \frac{Cov(X,Y)}{\sigma_X . \sigma_Y} \quad (1)$$

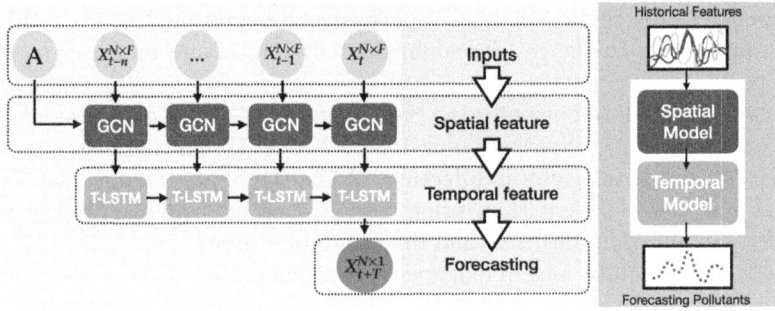

Fig. 1. Overview of *Graph Temporal LSTM* (GT-LSTM) comprising Spatial and Temporal Models. GCN and T-LSTM, respectively, are shown as the main components

Air pollution information within the network is represented by a feature matrix, denoted as **X**. This matrix has dimensions $N \times F \times t$, where N is the number of nodes (monitoring stations), F is the number of features (e.g., pollutant concentrations, meteorological data), and t is the time step. By structuring the data in this way, we can effectively analyze and model the relationships between air pollution levels, node attributes, and temporal patterns within the network.

Spatiotemporal air pollution forecasting involves learning a mapping function f that predicts future air pollution levels given a stationary network topology G and a feature matrix **X**. The goal is to predict air pollution levels for the next T time steps. The output, denoted as $\mathbf{X}_{t+T}^{N \times M}$, represents the predicted air pollution levels for all N nodes over the next T time steps. In this study, we focus on predicting $PM_{2.5}$ concentrations, setting $M = 1$. However, the proposed framework can be extended to multiple pollutants, treating M as the number of output variables, thereby enabling a multi-task learning approach.

The relationship depicted in our work is formalized by Eq. 2:

$$X_{t+1}^{N \times 1}, ..., X_{t+T}^{N \times 1} = f(G, X_{t-n}^{N \times F}, ..., X_{t-1}^{N \times F}, X_t^{N \times F}) \tag{2}$$

Figure 1 illustrates the implementation details of our framework, incorporating the parameters described earlier. The figure presents the architecture and modules of our model, demonstrating how the various elements interact to forecast future air pollutant levels. Each component will be elaborated upon in the following sections.

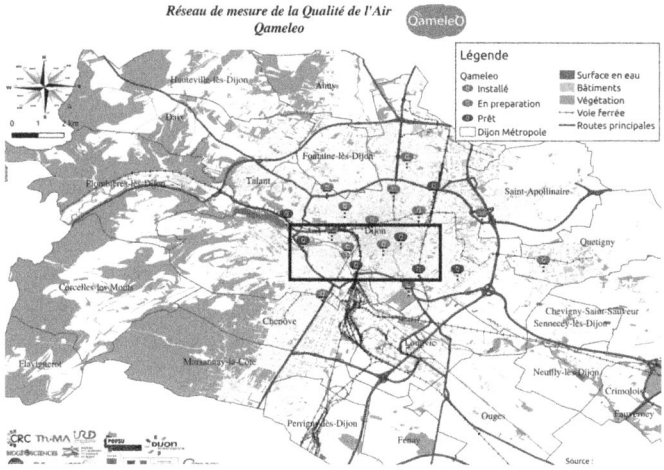

Fig. 2. Locations of Air Pollution Monitoring Stations in Dijon. The blue circles correspond to the active stations used in this study [21]. (Color figure online)

3.1 Graph Temporal LSTM (GT-LSTM)

To effectively capture both spatial and temporal dependencies among monitoring stations, we propose a novel spatiotemporal model termed GT-LSTM. Our study focuses on four monitoring stations within the air pollution network of Dijon, France: Canal, Hoche, Carnot, and Janin, designated as node 1 to node 4, respectively. Figure 2 provides a visual representation of the spatial distribution of the sensors deployed or soon to be deploy in this city. Data from the four blue sites in the black box are included in this study.

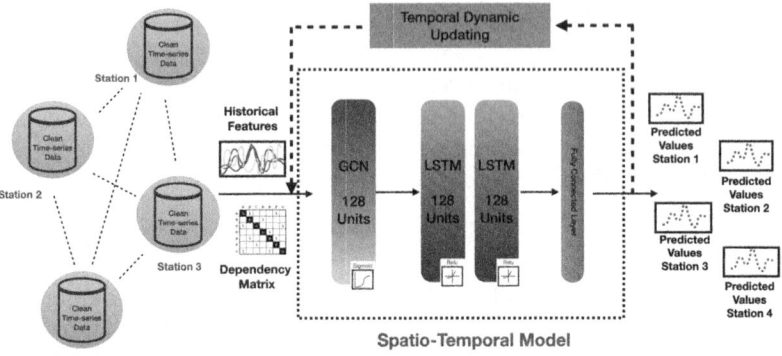

Fig. 3. Proposed spatiotemporal model. The model incorporates GCN blocks for capturing spatial features, LSTM blocks for capturing temporal features, temporal dynamic updating blocks, input data, a dependency matrix representing spatial relationships, and the predicted outputs.

3.2 Spatial Model

When it comes to predicting air pollution in an urban area, efficient topological resolution is essential. Relying on a single measurement in a city is often insufficient, particularly in larger cities. Therefore, to ensure accurate and comprehensive prediction, it is crucial to consider multiple measurements distributed throughout the urban area, motivating this study to have sub-zones for monitoring. To extract spatial data from a graph using a neural network, we employ GCN, which is an extension of CNN specifically designed to handle diverse graph-structured data [6]. In GCN, the process involves multiplying the input neurons by a set of weights, known as *filters* or *kernels*. These filters act as a sliding window across the entire data, allowing GCN to learn the characteristics of neighboring nodes within the graph. As described earlier, we effectively capture and learn spatial information from the graph structure. A GCN takes:

- an input feature matrix $N \times F$ feature matrix, X, where N is the number of nodes and F is the number of input features for each node, and
- an $N \times N$ matrix representation of the graph structure, such as the adjacency matrix A of G.

Figure 3 visually depicts the spatial distribution of the four monitoring stations and the proposed model architecture. The figure highlights how data from these stations are used to predict air quality at four different locations within the network topology and illustrates the model's capability to capture temporal dynamics. The model is lightweight, featuring one GCN layer with 128 units and two LSTM layers with 128 units each.

3.3 Temporal Model

To capture temporal dependencies, we employ an optimized LSTM model, termed *Temporal LSTM* (T-LSTM), as detailed in our previous work [28]. This lightweight and compact model has proven effective for various nodes. The comprehensive framework of PMForecast designed for air pollution prediction is outlined, comprising four key steps: data pre-processing, temporal attention to mitigate gradient disappearance, a flexible prediction horizon for dynamic future forecasting, and layers employing Long Short-Term Memory (LSTM)-the trainable component. The temporal attention prediction horizon mechanisms are encapsulated in the block *Temporal Dynamic Updating* in Fig. 3. This block is responsible for using temporal features such as the day of the week and also adjusting the prediction horizon for longer future forecasts. The LSTM model captures the temporal variations in the data, while the GCN model takes into account the topological structure and dependencies of the nodes.

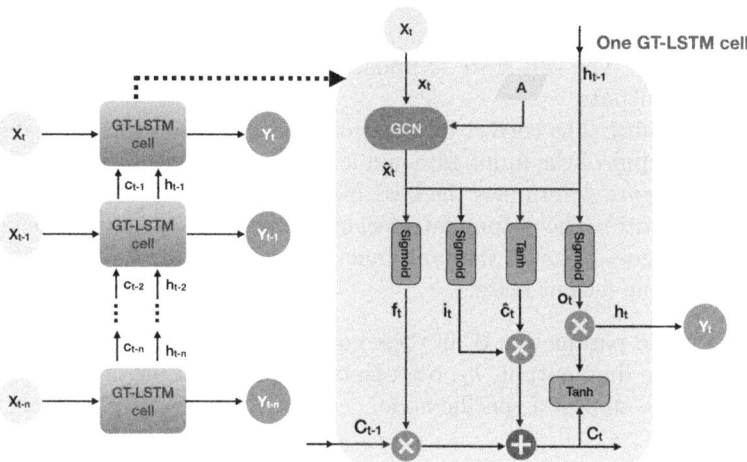

Fig. 4. A Cell of GT-LSTM

Figure 4 illustrates the architecture of a single GT-LSTM cell. The computational process within this cell is outlined by Eqs. 3 to 9. The GCN component, represented by Eq. 3, processes input features x through the adjacency matrix A to generate spatial embeddings $\hat{x}_t$. The LSTM component, defined by Eqs. 4 to 9, captures temporal dependencies through the calculation of different gates:

$$\hat{x}_t = \sigma(W_g \cdot x_t \cdot A + b_g) \tag{3}$$

$$f_t = \sigma(W_f \cdot [h_{t-1}, \hat{x}_t] + b_f) \tag{4}$$

$$i_t = \sigma(W_i \cdot [h_{t-1}, \hat{x}_t] + b_i) \tag{5}$$

$$\tilde{c}_t = \tanh(W_c \cdot [h_{t-1}, \hat{x}_t] + b_c) \tag{6}$$

$$c_t = f_t \odot c_{t-1} + i_t \odot \tilde{c}_t \tag{7}$$

$$o_t = \sigma(W_o \cdot [h_{t-1}, \hat{x}_t] + b_o) \tag{8}$$

$$h_t = o_t \odot \tanh(c_t) \tag{9}$$

- $\hat{x}_t$ (GCN-transformed features): Updates node features by aggregating neighboring information via the normalized adjacency matrix $\tilde{A}$, and applying a non-linear activation σ.
- f_t (forget gate): Decides whether the information can pass through different layers of the network. It takes input from the previous hidden state h_{t-1} and the current input $\hat{x}_t$.
- i_t (input gate): Determines the importance of the information by updating the cell state. It measures the integrity and importance of the information for developing predictions. The information passes through the sigmoid and tanh functions; the tanh eliminates the bias of the network, and the sigmoid determines the weight of the information.
- $\tilde{c}_t$ (cell state candidate): Represents the new candidate values that could be added to the cell state.
- c_t (cell state): The cell state is updated by combining the forget gate and input gate outputs.
- o_t (output gate): The correct information passes through the cell state. Once here, the output of the input gate and forget gate is multiplied by each other. The output gate determines the next hidden state of the network.
- h_t (hidden state): The output gate decides the next hidden state. The updated cell state c_t goes through the tanh function and is multiplied by the sigmoid function of the output state.

The weighted parameters W in these equations are learned during the training process. The final output, h_t, represents the predicted air pollution level for the current time step at a specific node.

4 Sensor Data Description and Pre-processing

In our study, we employed data collected from advanced air quality microstations, called 'QameleO', developed by the University of Burgundy [21]. QameleO is an affordable micro-station for monitoring air quality, developed collaboratively by two research teams from the University of Burgundy and the *Institut de Recherches pour le Développement* (IRD). The QameleO network was deployed to augment the existing air quality reference network operated by ATMO *Bourgogne Franche Comté* (ATMO-BFC) in the Dijon Metropolis. This reference network has been managed by regional governments since the 1990s. These micro-stations were deployed as part of the POPSU (*Plateforme d'Observation et de Stratégies Urbaines*) program within the Metropolis framework. Four locations (Port du Canal, Hoche, Carnot, and Janin) were selected to encompass various urban conditions, encompassing differing levels of traffic, background pollution, and intermediary scenarios. The dataset covered a period of one year, spanning from November 2020 to October 2021.

The data utilized in our analysis was collected at 15-minute intervals and encompassed five distinct measurements, including levels of particulate matters (PM_{10}, $PM_{2.5}$, PM_1), alongside meteorological variables : temperature and relative humidity. The QameleO dataset underwent comprehensive cleaning using advanced statistical algorithms at the University of Burgundy.

4.1 Data Acquisition and Preliminary Processing

The QameleO micro-station underwent thorough testing, encompassing both laboratory and outdoor evaluations, as part of a national air quality monitoring initiative led by INERIS (*Institut National de l'Environnement Industriel et des Risques*) and IMT (*Institut Mines Télécom*) Lille Douai, under the LCSQA (*Laboratoire Central de Surveillance de la Qualité de l'Air*). These assessments affirmed that the QameleO micro-station accurately captures the temporal variations in PMs mass concentrations. Measurements from QameleO micro-stations are captured every minute and then aggregated into 15-minute intervals to synchronize with the time-step of the ATMO reference stations deployed in Dijon Metropolis.

The data sets underwent various preprocessing stages as described in our previous work [28]. These stages included converting data from quarterly to hourly intervals. Then, we applied a moving average to effectively manage missing data and improve overall data quality. We utilized a sliding window technique with a 12-hour interval for each data point. Time-related features, such as day of the week and hour of the day, were integrated into the datasets, followed by normalization of values between zero and one. For a comprehensive understanding of this preprocessing pipeline, please refer to our prior study [28].

5 Experimental Results and Discussion

5.1 Model Performance Evaluation and Analysis

To evaluate the model's performance, we employed a combination of visual and quantitative analysis.

We visualized the correlation between observed and predicted values for the test sets, using density plots smoothed with a Gaussian kernel function (cf. Figure 5). Solid and dashed lines represent the true and predicted values, respectively, with colors corresponding to the four monitoring sites: Canal (red), Hoche (green), Carnot (orange), and Janin (purple). The close alignment between the curves demonstrates the model's strong predictive accuracy and consistency across all locations. The Gaussian distribution curve further emphasizes the model's accuracy, with its peak closely aligning with the predicted values, as represented by the dashed lines in the graph.

To further evaluate the model's ability to capture spatial dependencies, we conducted a detailed analysis focusing on two closely located sites (2 km apart):

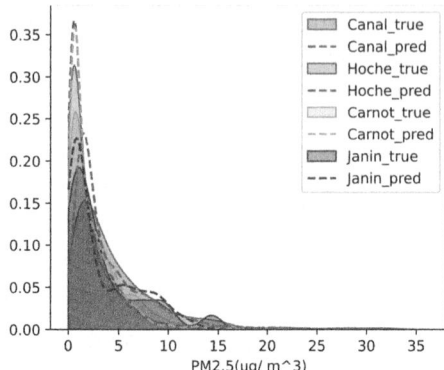

Fig. 5. Examination of the correlation between observed and predicted values for the test sets, smoothed using a Gaussian kernel function. The ground truth and predicted values are shown with solid and dashed lines, respectively. Colors represent the four sites in our datasets: Canal (red), Hoche (green), Carnot (orange), and Janin (purple). (Color figure online)

Hoche and Canal. The model effectively identifies similar air pollution patterns at these locations and produces consistent forecasting behaviors for both sites as it is shown in Fig. 6.

5.2 Evaluating the Model's Ability to Capture Spatiotemporal Patterns

One of the primary objectives of this study is to generate predicted values for various nodes by inputting different datasets into the model, with a particular focus on the $PM_{2.5}$. We provide compelling evidence that leveraging spatiotemporal modeling, which considers dependencies between nodes, enables accurate forecasting of pollution levels. This assertion is supported by results from four monitoring sites and notably Node 4 at the *Janin*. Indeed, despite unavailability of measurements at that site for a certain period in the test set, our model predicted the $PM_{2.5}$ values for this site based on other site predictions and dependencies between all of them. Figure 7 illustrates the test-set data for all nodes, with the *Janin* site highlighted in the lower-right section of the graph. This achievement demonstrates the model's ability to capture spatiotemporal relationships and deliver reliable forecasts, even when actual measurements are missing. It also reflects the model's consistent performance across different air pollutants.

A additional test was conducted to assess the stability of the model by artificially set Carnot site data to zero for the test set and predicting $PM_{2.5}$ values for all four nodes. Figure 8 illustrates both scenarios for the test set at the Carnot site: with real measurements and inputs set at zero. For Carnot, the predicted $PM_{2.5}$ values in both scenarios are similar and captured the ground truth data patterns well. However, the results show that in the scenario without background pollution, and intermediary scenarios. The dataset covered a period of one year, spanning from November 2020 to October 2021.

The data utilized in our analysis was collected at 15-minute intervals and encompassed five distinct measurements, including levels of particulate matters (PM_{10}, $PM_{2.5}$, PM_1), alongside meteorological variables : temperature and relative humidity. The QameleO dataset underwent comprehensive cleaning using advanced statistical algorithms at the University of Burgundy.

4.1 Data Acquisition and Preliminary Processing

The QameleO micro-station underwent thorough testing, encompassing both laboratory and outdoor evaluations, as part of a national air quality monitoring initiative led by INERIS (*Institut National de l'Environnement Industriel et des Risques*) and IMT (*Institut Mines Télécom*) Lille Douai, under the LCSQA (*Laboratoire Central de Surveillance de la Qualité de l'Air*). These assessments affirmed that the QameleO micro-station accurately captures the temporal variations in PMs mass concentrations. Measurements from QameleO micro-stations are captured every minute and then aggregated into 15-minute intervals to synchronize with the time-step of the ATMO reference stations deployed in Dijon Metropolis.

The data sets underwent various preprocessing stages as described in our previous work [28]. These stages included converting data from quarterly to hourly intervals. Then, we applied a moving average to effectively manage missing data and improve overall data quality. We utilized a sliding window technique with a 12-hour interval for each data point. Time-related features, such as day of the week and hour of the day, were integrated into the datasets, followed by normalization of values between zero and one. For a comprehensive understanding of this preprocessing pipeline, please refer to our prior study [28].

5 Experimental Results and Discussion

5.1 Model Performance Evaluation and Analysis

To evaluate the model's performance, we employed a combination of visual and quantitative analysis.

We visualized the correlation between observed and predicted values for the test sets, using density plots smoothed with a Gaussian kernel function (cf. Figure 5). Solid and dashed lines represent the true and predicted values, respectively, with colors corresponding to the four monitoring sites: Canal (red), Hoche (green), Carnot (orange), and Janin (purple). The close alignment between the curves demonstrates the model's strong predictive accuracy and consistency across all locations. The Gaussian distribution curve further emphasizes the model's accuracy, with its peak closely aligning with the predicted values, as represented by the dashed lines in the graph.

To further evaluate the model's ability to capture spatial dependencies, we conducted a detailed analysis focusing on two closely located sites (2 km apart):

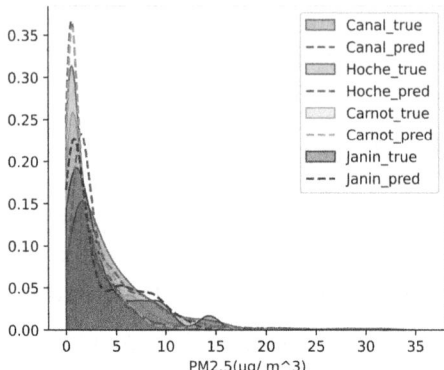

Fig. 5. Examination of the correlation between observed and predicted values for the test sets, smoothed using a Gaussian kernel function. The ground truth and predicted values are shown with solid and dashed lines, respectively. Colors represent the four sites in our datasets: Canal (red), Hoche (green), Carnot (orange), and Janin (purple). (Color figure online)

Hoche and Canal. The model effectively identifies similar air pollution patterns at these locations and produces consistent forecasting behaviors for both sites as it is shown in Fig. 6.

5.2 Evaluating the Model's Ability to Capture Spatiotemporal Patterns

One of the primary objectives of this study is to generate predicted values for various nodes by inputting different datasets into the model, with a particular focus on the $PM_{2.5}$. We provide compelling evidence that leveraging spatiotemporal modeling, which considers dependencies between nodes, enables accurate forecasting of pollution levels. This assertion is supported by results from four monitoring sites and notably Node 4 at the *Janin*. Indeed, despite unavailability of measurements at that site for a certain period in the test set, our model predicted the $PM_{2.5}$ values for this site based on other site predictions and dependencies between all of them. Figure 7 illustrates the test-set data for all nodes, with the *Janin* site highlighted in the lower-right section of the graph. This achievement demonstrates the model's ability to capture spatiotemporal relationships and deliver reliable forecasts, even when actual measurements are missing. It also reflects the model's consistent performance across different air pollutants.

A additional test was conducted to assess the stability of the model by artificially set Carnot site data to zero for the test set and predicting $PM_{2.5}$ values for all four nodes. Figure 8 illustrates both scenarios for the test set at the Carnot site: with real measurements and inputs set at zero. For Carnot, the predicted $PM_{2.5}$ values in both scenarios are similar and captured the ground truth data patterns well. However, the results show that in the scenario without

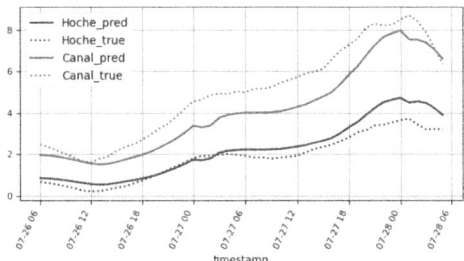

Fig. 6. Observed and predicted values for the Canal and Hoche sites over two days. Dotted lines represent the true values, while solid lines indicate the predicted values. The Hoche data is shown in blue, and the Canal data is shown in red. (Color figure online)

real measurements (called zero), the range of predicted $PM_{2.5}$ values is narrower in comparison to the classic scenario with real inputs (see Fig. 8 on the right). This indicates the model's limitation in distinguishing outliers when no actual input is provided, which is expected since the model lacks the historical data to predict values accurately. For the three other sites, there was a slight increase in error.

It is important to note that, in contrast, the temporal model [28] is unable to predict meaningful values when fed with zero or corrupted measurements. Instead, it either predicts zero or simply mirrors the flawed input data, relying exclusively on the data from the single station.

5.3 Assessing Model Capability for Long-Horizon Forecasting

Our forecasting model strongly predicts air pollution levels over extended time spans. Table 1 presents error and correlation metrics for test set across various time intervals, ranging from 1 h to 36 h into the future. These values represent the average of $PM_{2.5}$ predictions across all nodes, aggregated for each specific forecast horizon.

In Table 1, the model shows notable error reduction within the training dataset, achieving an average *Root Mean Square Error* (RMSE) value of 2.195 for the first 12 h in the test set. This indicates a significant correlation between predicted and actual values. The model also exhibits robust performance on the independent test dataset, with an average *Mean Absolute Error* (MAE) value of 1.277, demonstrating its ability to generalize effectively and provide reliable predictions even for unforeseen data beyond the 12-hour mark.

Table 1 evaluates the model's accuracy over longer forecast horizons. After 24 h, the accuracy of predictions decreases by more than 50%. Despite this, the model's performance indicates that extending forecasts beyond this period presents challenges. To improve long-term prediction quality, especially with large datasets, it is recommended to consider daily average predictions after the 24-hour mark.

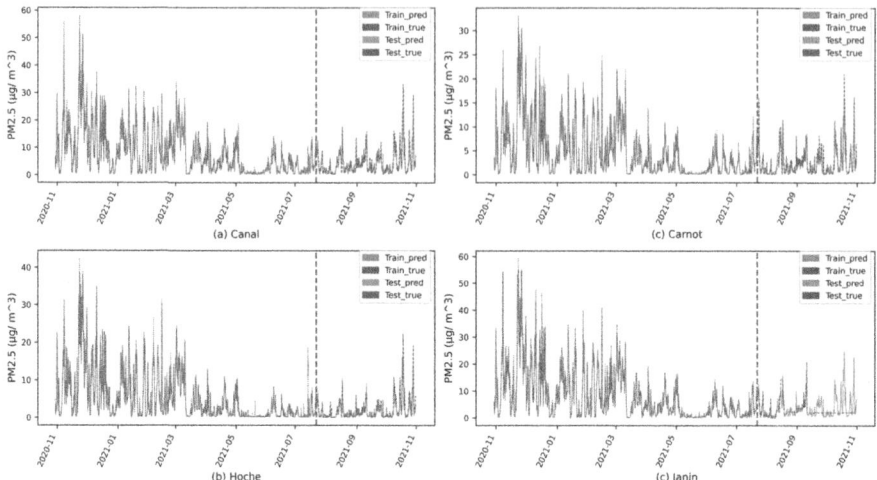

Fig. 7. Illustrating Model Robustness: predictions for all locations. The dashed lines represent the collected data, reflecting the actual values during both the training (blue) and prediction (golden) phases. The solid lines depict the $PM_{2.5}$ predictions made during the training (salmon) and prediction (green) phases. The vertical green dashed line marks the boundary between the training and testing datasets. (Color figure online)

Table 1. Evaluation Metrics for 1 to 36 h Forecasting

Hour(s)	RMSE	MAE	MSE	WMAPE (%)	R^2
1 h	1.433	0.786	2.138	18.3	0.892
6 h	1.702	1.001	3.103	28.7	0.811
12 h	2.195	1.277	5.360	35.2	0.643
24 h	2.635	1.429	8.197	47.5	0.458
36 h	3.112	1.712	10.569	59.1	0.356

5.4 Comparison of Local and Network-Based Forecasting Models

In this section, we analyze and compare key characteristics of the temporal model (PMForecast) [28] and the proposed spatiotemporal model GT-LSTM. PMForecast, which has shown strong predictive performance against baselines such as GRU and XGBoost, serves as the backbone for the temporal component of GT-LSTM. Building on this foundation, GT-LSTM incorporates spatial dependencies to enhance forecasting across multiple locations.

As detailed in Table 2, we evaluate both models across four dimensions: performance, computational efficiency, scalability, and data privacy. PMForecast demonstrates very high predictive accuracy (MAE: 0.164, Accuracy: 98%) but is limited to forecasting at a single station, with notable degradation when scaling to multiple sites. In contrast, GT-LSTM achieves high overall performance

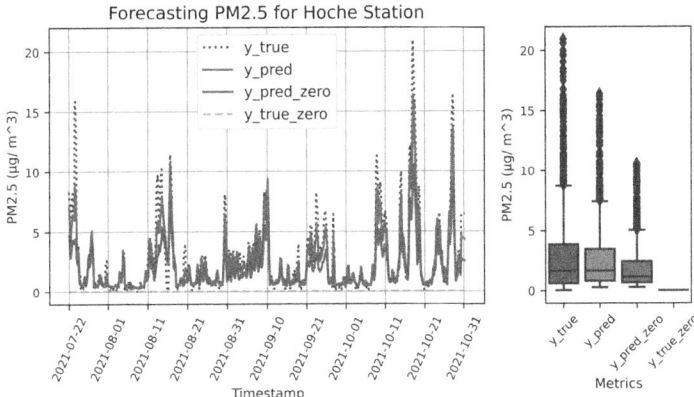

Fig. 8. Assessing Model Robustness: Two testing scenarios are considered. (i) Without Real Measurements (Using Zero Values): The dashed orange line represents zero values as input, while the solid green line shows the predicted values for this scenario. (ii) With Real Ground-Truth Measurements: The dotted blue line represents the actual ground-truth values, and the solid red line depicts the $PM_{2.5}$ predictions made using the real measurements for this scenario. (Color figure online)

(MAE: 0.786, Accuracy: 89%) while offering strong scalability-maintaining prediction quality across multiple monitoring stations without significant loss in accuracy. Although both models exhibit low computational efficiency, GT-LSTM is more efficient in terms of broader coverage, training on four stations in the same time PMForecast trains on one.

With respect to data privacy, both models rely on basic handling without encryption, highlighting an important limitation for deployment in sensitive or

Table 2. Comparison of Temporal and Spatio-Temporal Forecasting Models

Dimension	PMForecast (Temporal Model)	GT-LSTM (Spatio-Temporal Model)
Performance	Very High — MAE: 0.164, Accuracy: 98%	High — MAE: 0.786, Accuracy: 89%
Computational Efficiency	Low — Train Full Model Time: 212 s for 1 station	Low — Train Full Model Time: 423 s for 4 stations
Scalability	Low — Limited to 1 station	High — Scales well to multiple stations
Data Privacy	Low — No encryption, basic data handling	Low — No encryption, basic data handling

regulated environments. Future work could address this gap through privacy-preserving approaches such as data anonymization or federated learning.

5.5 Experimental Setup

The performance of deep learning models is highly influenced by hyperparameters such as learning rate, batch size, number of epochs, and hidden layer size. In this study, we performed limited but targeted hyperparameter tuning to identify configurations that provide stable performance without overfitting.

For the GCN component, we evaluated hidden unit sizes of [32, 64, 128, 256], with 128 units yielding the most consistent results. Among tested configurations, a single-layer GCN with Sigmoid activation provided the best trade-off between performance and complexity. This setup was effective in capturing local spatial relationships based on the available sensor data.

The temporal component followed the structure used in our prior work, which we found to be adequate for this dataset. It consists of two stacked LSTM layers, each with 128 units, using ReLU activation. This configuration offered a good balance between model capacity and computational efficiency.

We trained the model using the Huber loss function, selected for its robustness to outliers while maintaining precision for small errors. The learning rate was set to 0.001, and training was performed over 200 epochs with early stopping based on validation loss to reduce overfitting risk.

Although the experimental setup is limited by the number of available sensors—potentially restricting generalization and spatial diversity—the chosen configuration aimed to ensure fair evaluation under data-constrained conditions. Future work will explore scaling to denser sensor networks and broader spatial settings.

6 Conclusion

In conclusion, this study presents a spatiotemporal model designed to predict $PM_{2.5}$ concentrations in urban and suburbans environments. This work extends our previously validated temporal model [28] by integrating spatial learning through GCN, resulting in improved accuracy under sparse sensor conditions. Leveraging a low-cost sensor network and advanced AI techniques, the model effectively captures spatial and temporal air pollution patterns while maintaining a lightweight and scalable architecture.

Beyond predictive accuracy, the model offers practical value for long-term planning and targeted forecasting in subregions with limited data. Its real-time monitoring capability supports policymakers and local communities, enhancing air quality management and contributing to better public health outcomes.

7 Future Work

As part of future work, we propose integrating mobile sensor networks to improve the spatiotemporal resolution of air pollution monitoring. Deploying mobile sensors across urban areas will facilitate the collection of high-resolution, localized air quality data, enabling more precise and adaptive forecasting. To preserve data privacy while supporting distributed model training, we also plan to incorporate federated learning into the framework.

Acknowledgement. This project is funded by the European Union's Horizon 2020 research and innovation program (Marie Sklodowska-Curie agreement No. 847568). The research is conducted with the *Centre de Recherche en Informatique, Signal et Automatique de Lille* (CRIStAL) in partnership with Inria Lille and the *Laboratoire d'Optique Atmosphérique* (LOA) at the University of Lille. Quality-checked QAMELEO data is provided by the University of Bourgogne under the RESPONSE H2020 program. The QAMELEO network in Dijon is funded by the Ministry of Ecological Transition, Territorial Cohesion, and Dijon Metropolis (POPSU PURE program) and installed in collaboration with the University of Bourgogne and *Institut de Recherches pour le Développement* (IRD), co-owners of the instruments (Creative Commons open source license since 2020). The implementation of the Graph Temporal LSTM model used in this work are publicly available at [27].

References

1. Alexander Baklanov, Y.Z.: Advances in air quality modeling and forecasting. Global Trans. **2**, 261–270 (2020). https://doi.org/10.1016/j.glt.2020.11.001
2. Belavadi, S.V., Rajagopal, S., Mohan, R.: Air quality forecasting using LSTM RNN and wireless sensor networks. Procedia Comput. Sci. **170**, 241–248 (2020). https://doi.org/10.1016/j.procs.2020.03.036, https://www.sciencedirect.com/science/article/pii/S1877050920304658
3. Deakin, E.: Sustainable development and sustainable transportation: strategies for economic prosperity, environmental quality, and equity. Technical report, UC Berkeley: Institute of Urban and Regional Development (2001). https://escholarship.org/uc/item/0m1047xc
4. Defferrard, M., Bresson, X., Vandergheynst, P.: Convolutional neural networks on graphs with fast localized spectral filtering. CoRR abs/1606.09375 (2016). http://arxiv.org/abs/1606.09375
5. Drewil, G.I., Al-Bahadili, R.J.: Air pollution prediction using LSTM deep learning and metaheuristics algorithms. Measur. Sens. **24**, 100546 (2022). https://doi.org/10.1016/j.measen.2022.100546
6. García-Duarte, L., Cifuentes, J., Marulanda, G.: Short-term spatio-temporal forecasting of air temperatures using deep graph convolutional neural networks. Stoch. Env. Res. Risk Assess. **37**(5), 1649–1667 (2023). https://doi.org/10.1007/s00477-022-02358-0
7. Ge, L., Wu, K., Zeng, Y., Chang, F., Wang, Y., Li, S.: Multi-scale spatiotemporal graph convolution network for air quality prediction. Appl. Intell. **51**(6), 3491–3505 (2021). https://doi.org/10.1007/s10489-020-02054-y
8. Ge, L., Wu, K., Zeng, Y., Chang, F., Wang, Y., Li, S.: Multi-scale spatiotemporal graph convolution network for air quality prediction. Appl. Intell. **51**(6), 3491–3505 (2021). https://doi.org/10.1007/S10489-020-02054-Y
9. Gilik, A., Ogrenci, A.S., Ozmen, A.: Air quality prediction using CNN+LSTM-based hybrid deep learning architecture. Environ. Sci. Pollut. Res. **29**(8), 11920–11938 (2022). https://doi.org/10.1007/s11356-021-16227-w

10. Gokul, P., Mathew, A., Bhosale, A., Nair, A.T.: Spatio-temporal air quality analysis and pm2.5 prediction over Hyderabad city, India using artificial intelligence techniques. Ecol. Inform. **76**, 102067 (2023). https://doi.org/10.1016/j.ecoinf.2023.102067, https://www.sciencedirect.com/science/article/pii/S1574954123000961
11. Guo, Z., et al.: Optimized air quality management based on air quality index prediction and air pollutants identification in representative cities in China. Sci. Rep. **14**(1), 17923 (2024). https://doi.org/10.1038/s41598-024-68972-w
12. He, Y., Ma, J., Zhang, C., Yang, H.: Spatio-temporal evolution and prediction of carbon storage in Guilin based on FLUS and InVEST models. Remote Sens. **15**, 1445. https://doi.org/10.3390/rs15051445
13. Hofman, J., et al.: Spatiotemporal air quality inference of low-cost sensor data: evidence from multiple sensor testbeds. Environ. Model. Softw. **149**, 105306 (2022). https://doi.org/10.1016/j.envsoft.2022.105306, https://www.sciencedirect.com/science/article/pii/S1364815222000123
14. Jain, A., Bhasin, A., Gupta, V.: Prediction of air pollution using LSTM-based recurrent neural networks. Int. J. Comput. Intell. Stud. **8**(4), 299–308 (2019). https://doi.org/10.1504/IJCISTUDIES.2019.103620
15. Kim, K.H., Kabir, E., Kabir, S.: A review on the human health impact of airborne particulate matter. Environ. Int. **74**, 136–143 (2015). https://doi.org/10.1016/j.envint.2014.10.005, https://www.sciencedirect.com/science/article/pii/S0160412014002992
16. Krzyzanowski, M., Apte, J.S., Bonjour, S.P., Brauer, M., Cohen, A.J., Prüss-Ustun, A.M.: Air pollution in the mega-cities. Technical report 3, Current Environmental Health Reports (2001). https://doi.org/10.1007/s40572-014-0019-7
17. Le, V.D.: Spatiotemporal graph convolutional recurrent neural network model for citywide air pollution forecasting (2023). https://arxiv.org/abs/2304.12630
18. Le, V.D., Bui, T.C., Cha, S.K.: Spatiotemporal deep learning model for citywide air pollution interpolation and prediction. In: 2020 IEEE International Conference on Big Data and Smart Computing (BigComp), pp. 55–62 (2020). https://doi.org/10.1109/BigComp48618.2020.00-99
19. Lee, H.M., et al.: Pm2.5 source attribution for Seoul in may from 2009 to 2013 using geos-chem and its adjoint model. Environmental Pollution **221**, 377–384 (2017). https://doi.org/10.1016/j.envpol.2016.11.088
20. M, D., V, R.: Novel regression and least square support vector machine learning technique for air pollution forecasting. CoRR abs/2306.07301 (2023). https://doi.org/10.48550/ARXIV.2306.07301
21. Martiny, N., et al.: Quality of air module for environmental learning engineering and observation network (qameleondijon) : un réseau dense de mesures de qualité de l'air à dijon», climatologie **20**(4) (2023). https://doi.org/10.1051/climat/202320004
22. Norby, R.J., Luo, Y.: Evaluating ecosystem responses to rising atmospheric co2 and global warming in a multi-factor world. New Phytol. **162**(2), 281–293 (2004). https://doi.org/10.1111/j.1469-8137.2004.01047.x
23. Organization, W.H.: Air pollution and child health. World Health Organization (2006)
24. Pak, U., et al.: Deep learning-based pm2.5 prediction considering the spatiotemporal correlations: a case study of Beijing, China. Sci. Total Environ. **699**, 133561 (2020). https://doi.org/10.1016/j.scitotenv.2019.07.367, https://www.sciencedirect.com/science/article/pii/S0048969719334813

25. Pakrooh, P., Pishbahar, E.: Forecasting air pollution concentrations in Iran, using a hybrid model. Pollution **5**(4), 739–747 (2019). https://doi.org/10.22059/poll.2019.274827.572
26. Qin, D., Yu, J., Zou, G., Yong, R., Zhao, Q., Zhang, B.: A novel combined prediction scheme based on CNN and LSTM for urban pm2.5 concentration. IEEE Access **7**, 20050–20059 (2019). https://doi.org/10.1109/ACCESS.2019.2897028
27. Rahmani, M.: Graph temporal LSTM for air quality forecasting. https://github.com/Maryamr92/GT-LSTM (2024). Accessed 08 Apr 2025
28. Rahmani, M., Crumeyrolle, S., Allegri-Martiny, N., Taherkordi, A., Rouvoy, R.: PMforecast: leveraging temporal LSTM to deliver in situ air quality predictions. Environ. Sci. Pollut. Res. (2024). https://doi.org/10.1007/s11356-024-34623-w
29. Shakir, M., Kumaran, U., Rakesh, N.: An approach towards forecasting time series air pollution data using LSTM-based auto-encoders. J. Internet Serv. Inf. Secur. **14**(2), 32–46 (2024). https://doi.org/10.58346/JISIS.2024.I2.003
30. Yin, L., Liu, P., Wu, Y., Shi, C., Wei, X., He, Y.: ST-VGBiGRU: A hybrid model for traffic flow prediction with spatio-temporal multimodality. IEEE Access **11**, 54968–54985. https://doi.org/10.1109/ACCESS.2023.3282323
31. Zhang, Q., Han, Y., Li, V., Lam, J.: Deep-air: a hybrid CNN-LSTM framework for fine-grained air pollution estimation and forecast in metropolitan cities. IEEE Access **10**, 55818–55841 (2022). https://doi.org/10.1109/ACCESS.2022.3174853

Justin: Hybrid CPU/Memory Elastic Scaling for Distributed Stream Processing

Donatien Schmitz[1](✉), Guillaume Rosinosky[2], and Etienne Rivière[1]

[1] ICTEAM, UCLouvain, Ottignies-Louvain-la-Neuve, Belgium
{donatien.schmitz,etienne.riviere}@uclouvain.be
[2] IMT Atlantique, Nantes Université, École Centrale Nantes, CNRS, Inria, LS2N - UMR 6004, Nantes, France
guillaume.rosinosky@inria.fr

Abstract. Distributed Stream Processing (DSP) engines analyze continuous data via queries expressed as a graph of operators. Auto-scalers adjust the number of parallel instances of these operators to support a target rate. Current auto-scalers couple CPU and memory scaling, allocating resources as one-size-fits-all packages. This contrasts with operators' high diversity of requirements.

We present Justin, an auto-scaler that enables hybrid CPU and memory scaling of DSP operators. Justin monitors both CPU usage and the performance of operators' storage operations. Its mechanisms enable fine-grain memory allocation for tasks upon a query reconfiguration. The Justin policy identifies individual operators' memory pressure and decides between adjusting parallelism and/or memory assignment. We implement Justin in Apache Flink, extending the Flink Kubernetes Operator and the DS2 CPU-only auto-scaler. Using the Nexmark benchmark, our evaluation shows that Justin identifies suitable resource allocation in as many or fewer reconfiguration steps as DS2 and supports a target rate with significantly fewer CPU and memory resources.

Keywords: Distributed Stream Processing · Resource Management · Elastic Scaling · Hybrid Scaling · Apache Flink

1 Introduction

Stream Processing allows continuous data analysis in a large variety of applications [14]. Supporting stream processing over large volumes of incoming data requires distributing computation over multiple machines. Distributed Stream Processing (DSP) engines, such as Apache Storm [2], Spark Streaming [38], or Apache Flink [1], emerged to address the many challenges associated with the distribution and orchestration of parallel stream processing. This includes fault tolerance [9], connection to input sources and destinations, and support for elastic scaling, i.e., the ability to dynamically adapt the amount of computational resources to sustainably support a target *rate* of input events.

Artifacts available in https://doi.org/10.5281/zenodo.15209785.

A stream processing query is a directed graph of *operators* performing computation on incoming events. Elastic scaling assigns, at runtime, each operator to several *tasks*, i.e., individual threads of execution. The flow of events is distributed to these tasks to be processed in parallel. Numerous auto-scalers have been proposed in the literature [10,28]. Apache Flink recently integrated a variant of the DS2 [17] auto-scaler in its Kubernetes Operator [3]. DS2 determines the processing capacity of tasks based on a measure of their *busyness*, the fraction of CPU time effectively spent processing events. It derives a new configuration mapping operators to a required number of tasks to sustain a target input rate while considering cascade effects between operators' loads.

Motivation. Existing auto-scalers couple CPU and memory allocation [9]. Scaling out an operator (i.e., adding more tasks) adds a proportional amount of memory. This coupled, one-size-fits-all allocation clashes with the heterogeneous memory requirements of operators. Some operators, such as a *filter* or a *map*, are stateless and do not require more than a minimal amount of memory to process events efficiently. In contrast, other operators, such as *joins* or *group by* over long windows, maintain state across the processing of many events [36].

Intuitively, stateful operators with under-allocating memory perform poorly: The necessary state may not fit in the main memory, and accesses may resort to on-disk storage. In contrast, ample memory allocation (e.g., as the operator has been scaled out to multiple tasks) should not yield better performance than a smaller but sufficient allocation.

In reality, the relation between event processing performance, state access latency, and memory requirements is more subtle than this simple intuition. State-of-the-art state backends for stream processing use a Log-Structured-Merge tree (LSM) [21,25]. An LSM combines tables and caches in memory with bulk storage on disk. They use optimizations to favor write performance and minimize the wear of modern SSD drives. For instance, Flink uses the LSM-based RocksDB [4,12] for production deployments. The performance in response to the available memory of RocksDB depends heavily on the nature of the workload [7]. Workloads formed mainly of *write* operations do not benefit from a large memory allocation. In contrast, workloads dependent on *read* operations do, in proportion to the size of their working set. The nature of an operator's access to its state is not predictable, as it often depends on the characteristics of its input events.

Contributions. We present Justin, a hybrid auto-scaler that considers *both* CPU and memory allocation when reconfiguring DSP queries. In contrast with previous approaches, Justin's auto-scaling policy can decide to scale *up* (i.e., adding more memory to each task) or scale *out* (adding more tasks) depending on runtime indicators on state access performance. We integrate Justin in Apache Flink and the Flink Kubernetes Operator [3], extending the current elastic scaling engine based on DS2 [17].

Our contributions and the outline of the remainder of this paper are as follows. We start with the necessary background and terminology about Flink (Sect. 2). We discuss state management and RocksDB and analyze, using

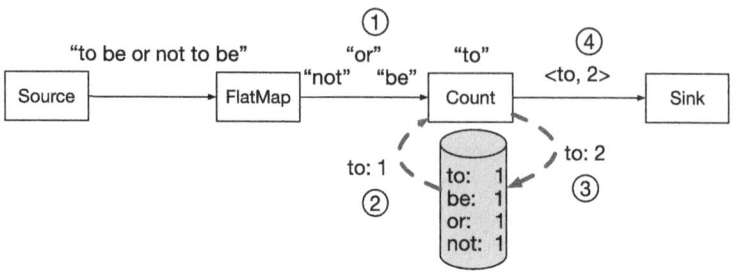

Fig. 1. A WordCount query using four operators.

microbenchmarks, the impact of workload characteristics on state lookup performance and response to memory availability (Sect. 3).

We then present Justin policies and mechanisms (Sect. 4). We detail DS2, Flink's current elastic scalers. We present how Justin collects metrics about a running query's resource usage and storage performance in RocksDB. Based on these metrics, Justin's auto-scaling policy adjusts DS2 decisions and derives CPU and memory allocations. These allocations are enacted by mechanisms for fine-grain resource allocation in Flink and the Flink Kubernetes Operator [3].

We evaluate Justin in Flink on a 7-node cluster under high loads and compare it to DS2 using the Nexmark benchmark [35] (Sect. 5). Our results show Justin produces configurations with 48% less CPU and 27–28% less memory for q8 and q11, two complex stateful queries while requiring the same or fewer reconfiguration steps than DS2.

We review related work on hybrid vertical/horizontal scaling (Sect. 6) and conclude the paper by identifying future directions (Sect. 7).

2 Background

We provide background information on stream processing. We use Flink's terminology but note that concepts are similar in other stream processing engines. We detail state management and elastic scaling in Sects. 3 and 4.

Stream Processing. A stream processing query is a dataflow graph where vertices are *operators* $o_i \in O$ and edges represent flows of events between these operators. Operators can support arbitrary computation but are often selected from a library of classical transformations or compiled from SQL [26].

Operators can be single-input, such as a *filter* (i.e., letting through a subset of events), a *map* (individual transformation of events), or a *group by* followed by aggregation. Others consume multiple streams, e.g., *joins*. Commonly, operators such as aggregates and *joins* compute over a *window* defined as a count of events or a period [36]. These operators are *stateful*: they must keep track of information related to events over this window. In contrast, operators that process events in isolation (*map*, *filter*, etc.) are *stateless*.

Word Count Example. Figure 1 presents *word count*, a classic example query implemented using three operators. This query counts occurrences of individual

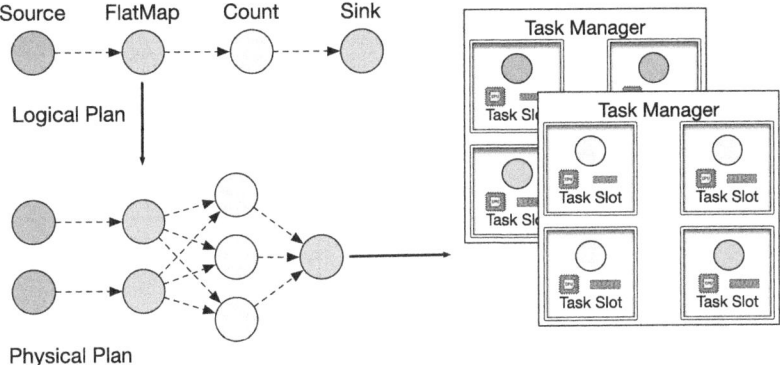

Fig. 2. Word count query deployed on two Task Managers and eight Task Slots.

words in a stream of sentences. The *Source* is a specific operator injecting sentences as new events, e.g., from disk or a stream store such as Apache Kafka [18]. A *FlatMap* operator splits these sentences into multiple events, one for each word (①). The *Count* operator combines a *group by* and a *sum* aggregate to count occurrences of each word over a time window. The processing of each event by this operator requires fetching the current count from the storage backend (②) and updating it (③). Finally, a *Sink* operator receives and stores outputs, e.g., to Kafka (④). In this example, the *Count* operator is stateful; others are stateless.

Query Execution. A query's logical plan is executed by a physical plan where each operator can be supported by several processing *tasks*, as illustrated by Fig. 2. Each task is a single thread of execution. The number of tasks of an operator is also denoted as its *parallelism*. In Flink, the execution of tasks is supported by a fleet of processes (Java Virtual Machines) called Task Managers (TMs) orchestrated by a centralized Job Manager (JM). Each TM has a predefined number of identical Task Slots (TSs). Each TS can run one task. CPU resources allocated to a TM are divided between its TSs. In this paper, we consider the standard one-core-per-task model. We discuss the allocation of TM memory in the next section and evaluate its impact on performance.

3 Impact of Memory on Operators' Performance

We study in this section the relationship between memory allocation and task performance in Flink. The takeaways of this section guide the design of our hybrid CPU/memory auto-scaler, Justin, detailed in the next section.

RocksDB. The state of stateful operators' tasks must be persisted across the processing of different events. The storage must allow for reconfiguration and restoration after failures [9]. Furthermore, this state may be arbitrarily large and not fit into memory. While an in-memory storage backend is available for testing in Flink, production deployments use RocksDB [4,12], a state backend using a Log Structured Merge (LSM) tree and offering a key/value interface.

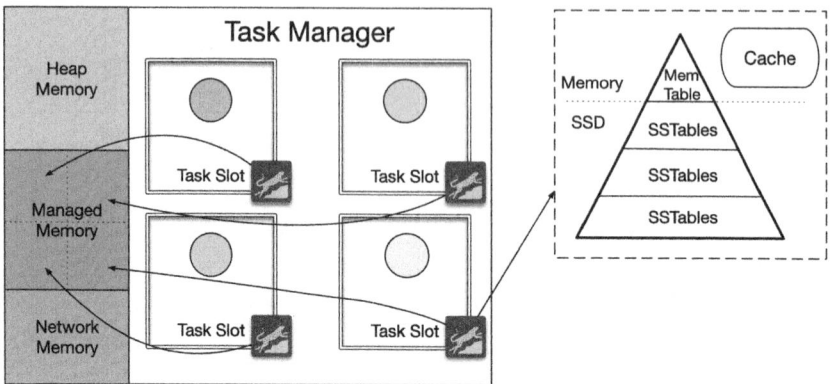

Fig. 3. Memory allocation between tasks and RocksDB LSM tree.

An LSM tree, illustrated on the right of Fig. 3, is a data structure optimized for write-heavy workloads and reducing wear on the storage device, typically an SSD. Writes are buffered in memory (in a MemTable) and later flushed to disk in sorted order, reducing random I/O. A hierarchy of sorted SSTables (Sorted String Tables) files is periodically merged into larger ones, reducing fragmentation and read amplification. Data is stored across multiple levels of this hierarchy, with newer data at higher levels and older data compacted into lower levels. As a result, reads may require searching SSTables across multiple levels, increasing their latency. To mask these costs, RocksDB uses an in-memory *cache* of recently accessed data.

The MemTable, implemented as a skip list, is used to buffer writes before consolidating them to SSTables. Using a large MemTable has no real impact on write latencies, as consolidation is performed at the granularity of the first-level SSTable (of 64 MB). In contrast, read latency is directly impacted by the size of the cache and its relation to the task's working set size (i.e., the set of keys the task frequently accesses over a period). Tasks performing frequent reads, as for the *Count* operator of the word count in Fig. 1, may have to resort to costly exploration of SSTables on disk if the cache is not large enough. Tasks performing only or mostly writes are not impacted by the cache size.

TM Memory Allocation. Memory sharing between TSs on the same TM depends on the JVM's memory segmentation. On-heap memory, used by Flink operators for creating Java objects and subject to garbage collection, is shared among all tasks. The same applies to network memory used for communication buffers. While there is no isolation between threads for access to these segments, a TM reserves a minimum amount for each TS. In contrast, *managed memory* is specific to a thread and is not subject to garbage collection. It is used by the RocksDB instance local to each task to store its MemTable and cache.

Takeaway 1. Managed memory is reserved for all task slots in equal amounts. This memory is wasted for stateless tasks that do not use RocksDB. Stateful tasks get a one-size-fits-all allocation, regardless of their requirements.

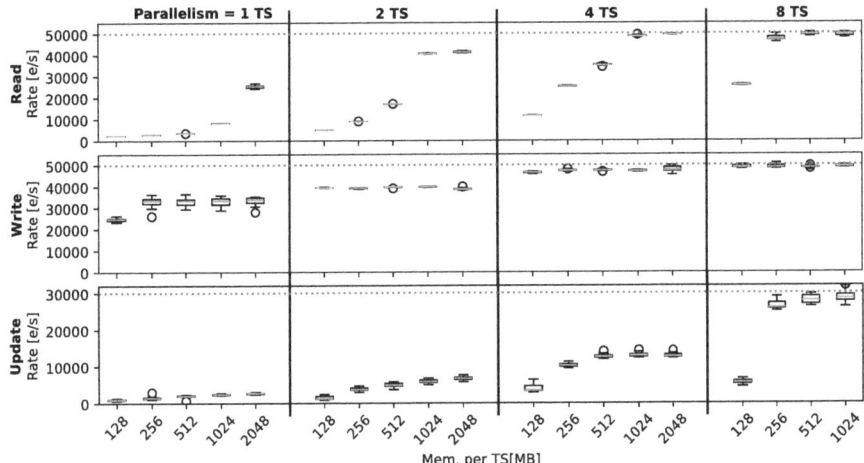

Fig. 4. Evaluation of multiple memory-cpu configurations on three different state access patterns. Benchmarks show the maximum rate reachable against a target rate (dotted line). The impact of memory on rate significantly differs depending on the workload, read-only being the more profitable.

Microbenchmarks. We evaluate the impact of memory allocation on performance using microbenchmarks. We use a single operator. The input stream is formed of events of 1,000 B. Each event includes a key generated uniformly at random between 0 and 1,000,000 and a random payload. The RocksDB state backend is pre-populated with a value associated with each key. We consider three workloads. In the **Read** workload, the operator reads the value associated with the key in the event. In the **Write** workload, it replaces the value associated with this key without reading the previous value. In the **Update** workload, the operator reads the current value and then overrides it with the event's payload. We use a target rate of 50,000 events per second for the Read and Write workloads and 30,000 events per second for the Update workload.

Our results are presented in Fig. 4. We consider 19 configurations for each workload, with an operator's parallelism ranging from 1 to 8 tasks and managed memory allocation of 128 to 2,048 MB. In any memory allocation, the MemTable size is at most 64 MB, and the rest is used for the cache. By default, Flink prioritizes the allocation of at least half of the memory to the cache, possibly reducing the size of the MemTable, which is allocated as a power-of-2 granularity. As a result, an allocation of 128 MB of memory results in a 32 MB MemTable and a 96 MB cache, but allocations of 256 MB or 512 MB result in a 64 MB Memtable and, respectively, 192 MB and 448 MB caches. We denote a configuration with t tasks and m MB of memory as $(t; m)$. We run each configuration for 10 min. We measure aggregate rate every 5 s and present the distribution as a box plot. The dotted line indicates the target rate. We use specific source operators that produce events at the maximal possible speed, subject to back pressure from the measured operator and capped by this target rate.

We observe that the target rate is sustained for the Read workload starting from (4; 1,024) or (8; 512). Below that, we observe that the cache hit rate (not shown on the plot) is very low, impacting processing time for every event. With 256 MB of memory, even the 8-task configuration is slightly below the target rate, possibly requiring further scale-out and the use of a lot of CPU resources.

Takeaway 2. Scaling out a read-intensive operator without appropriate memory allocation can lead to inefficient scale-out operations. The cache hit rate is a key metric for determining when the cache size is insufficient and scaling up.

The Write workload shows constant performance at all parallelisms with all memory configurations, except the smallest (1; 128), which is slightly below (1; 256). This lower performance is due to the smaller MemTable size. The target rate is reached with a parallelism of 8, with 4 tasks being very close.

Takeaway 3. The size of the cache does not impact write performance. Write-dominated operators should favor scale-out to scale-in.

Finally, the evaluation of the Update workload shows that only an 8-task configuration can sustain the workload. We also observe a *plateau* effect for 4 and 8 tasks, where adding memory does not result in significant gains (in contrast with the Read workload, where these gains are more linear). Configurations with insufficient memory (128 MB) cannot sustain the rate regardless of parallelism.

Takeaway 4. It is necessary to vertically scale (add memory) above a minimum threshold. If a scale-up does not improve performance significantly, it is preferable to scale out.

4 Justin: Hybrid CPU/memory Auto-Scaler

Building upon the takeaways of the previous section, we design Justin as a hybrid auto-scaler that decides on scaling *up* or scaling *out* an operator depending on its needs and avoids allocating memory to tasks that do not need or use it. Justin builds upon DS2 [17], Flink's current auto-scaler. We start with a recap of DS2 principles. Then, we detail the metrics collected by Justin. We present an auto-scaling policy that uses these metrics and explain how we enable dynamic, heterogeneous memory allocation for tasks.

Elastic Scaling and DS2. Elastic scaling determines the appropriate level of parallelism for all operators. From a default configuration (parallelism of tasks and memory per task) at time $t = 0$, reconfigurations are triggered, based on observations, at discrete times $t > 0$. We define a configuration C^t as a map between operators $o_i \in O$ where $o_i.p^t$ is the parallelism p (number of tasks) of operator i at time t.

DS2 [17] uses a primary metric, the busyness of operators, averaged across their tasks. Busyness is the fraction of CPU time spent processing events, i.e., not idling or waiting due to back pressure. A reconfiguration trigger is a high busyness for one of its operators in addition to backpressure from its upstream operator(s), indicating that the query's capacity is insufficient to cope with the current rate. When triggered at time t, DS2 determines a new level of parallelism $o_i.p^t$ for each operator such that the resulting busy rate is below a target. For this purpose, it uses linearity assumptions and considers that the load will be equally distributed among the scaled-out operator's tasks. This computation accounts for the cascade effects between operators: scaling out an operator increases its capacity, resulting in a higher rate for downstream operators and the need to scale them out as well. The new configuration is applied via a query reconfiguration, possibly resulting in state transfers between RocksDB instances [9]. DS2 typically requires several reconfiguration steps until it reaches a stable configuration for a target rate, and setting appropriate thresholds for triggering reconfiguration and target busyness levels requires careful tuning.

Integrating Memory-Awareness. Justin requires memory-centric indicators in addition to CPU ones, such as busyness. We note, however, that there can be a coupling between memory and CPU indicators. A task performing high-latency state accesses may have a high busyness, as state accesses are accounted for as part of the event processing time. State access latency allows distinguishing between the two cases. High average access latency $o_i.\tau^t$ indicates that a significant fraction of accesses by o_i's tasks used the disk and that scaling out may not be the best option until the cache is appropriately dimensioned. Furthermore, RocksDB exports the number of cache hits and misses, from which we can derive an average *cache hit rate* $o_i.\theta^t$ for operator o_i's tasks. We collect these two metrics using Prometheus [11]. As for other metrics, these are collected and averaged over a period.

4.1 Justin Policy Building BLocks

The elastic scaling policy of Justin extends DS2, specifically its implementation in Flink and the associated Kubernetes support operator [3]. This choice allows building upon the complex engineering, integration, and parameter tuning already made by the open-source community and improves impact potential.

Memory Allocation. Justin allocates heterogeneous memory to the tasks of different operators. $o_i.m^t$ represents in a configuration C^t the managed memory, in MB, allocated to all tasks of an operator o_i. To facilitate the mapping of tasks to task managers, we allocate memory in *levels*. Each new level corresponds to double per-task memory, from a minimum to a maximum (*maxLevel*). For $o_i.m^t = x$, we allocate 2^x times the minimum of managed memory for stateful tasks. If, for instance, the minimum managed memory is 128 MB, $o_i.m^t = 0$ means 128 MB, $o_i.m^t = 1$ means 256 MB, etc. Stateless tasks are allocated no managed memory, expressed as $o_i.m^t = \bot$.

Decisions History. DS2 does not maintain a history of scaling decisions, as it only takes these in one direction (horizontally). In contrast, Justin can choose between scaling out or up. Keeping a decision history helps determine whether they improved the query capacity. Past configurations are available in $C^0 \ldots C^{t-1}$. A boolean $o_i.v^t$ indicates that, in C^t, the scaling decision involved *scaling up* (vertically) the memory of operator o_i's tasks (i.e., $o_i.v^t = \top \implies o_i.m^t > o_i.m^{t-1}$).

4.2 Justin Policy Algorithm

Algorithm 1 is called when the capacity of the query is insufficient and requires a reconfiguration. We use the unmodified DS2 trigger based on busyness and backpressure metrics.

Algorithm 1: Justin's hybrid elastic scaling policy

Parameters: $\Delta_\theta \leftarrow 80\%$; $\Delta_\tau \leftarrow 1ms$; $maxLevel \leftarrow 3$
Result: A new configuration C^t

1 $C^t \leftarrow DS2()$ // Obtain initial configuration from DS2
2 **for** $o_i \in C^t$ **do**   // Iterate over all operators
3   **if** o_i is stateless   // No recorded RocksDB access?
4        $o_i.m^t \leftarrow \perp$ // Disable managed memory for o_i
5   **else**
6   **if** $o_i.p^t \neq o_i.p^{t-1}$ // o_i's capacity insufficient?
7   **if** $o_i.v^{t-1}$ // Vertical scaling used last time?
8   **if** $(o_i.\theta^t > o_i.\theta^{t-1} \lor o_i.\tau^t < o_i.\tau^{t-1})$ // Did it improve?
9   **if** $(o_i.m^{t-1} + 1) < maxLevel$ // Can scale-up?
10                   $o_i.p^t \leftarrow o_i.p^{t-1}$ // Cancel scale out
11                   $o_i.m^t \leftarrow o_i.m^{t-1} + 1$ // Increase memory further
12                   $o_i.v^t \leftarrow True$
13   **else**   // Did not improve?
14                $o_i.m^t \leftarrow o_i.m^{t-1} - 1$ // Roll-back scale in
15   **else**
16   **if** $(o_i.\theta^t < \Delta_\theta \lor o_i.\tau^t > \Delta_\tau) \land o_i.m^{t-1} + 1 < maxLevel$
                                           // Could vertical scaling be useful?
17                $o_i.p^t \leftarrow o_i.p^{t-1}$ // Cancel scale out
18                $o_i.m^t \leftarrow o_i.m^{t-1} + 1$ // Attempt increasing memory
19                $o_i.v^t \leftarrow True$
20 **return** C^t // Return the updated configuration

The key principle of Justin's policy is, in appropriate situations, to prioritize a vertical scaling action to a horizontal scaling action decided by DS2. It uses memory efficiency metrics to determine if there is a gain potential and leverages insights from past scaling decisions to evaluate whether they improved capacity. The policy starts by calling the unmodified DS2 (Line 1). It then iterates over all operators. It first identifies if the operator is stateless, which is indicated by the absence of RocksDB-specific metrics in Prometheus (Line 3). If it is, we remove its portion of managed memory (Line 4) and keep the parallelism given by DS2.

For stateful operators, we consider those where a re-scaling decision is proposed by DS2 (Line 6). Other operators' capacities are deemed sufficient and do not need to scale. We then distinguish between two cases: if the operator was vertically scaled the previous time (Lines 7–14) or not (Lines 16–19).

If the operator was previously scaled up, we determine if this led to an improvement. As discussed in Sect. 3, this depends on the number of writes vs. reads, the size of the working set, among other factors. A scaled-up operator that does not give better capacity is unlikely to improve with further scale-up. We assess this improvement by comparing the cache hit ratio and state access latency of the current and previous periods (Line 8).[1] If there was an improvement and the operator is not already at the maximum memory level, we cancel the scale-out (Line 10) and replace it with scale-up (Line 11). If there was no improvement, we cancel the previous scale-up (Line 14) to avoid wasting memory. The parallelism recommended by DS2 will thus apply using the previous memory configuration.

If an operator was not scaled up already (or was so earlier than $t-1$), we evaluate if the cache hit rate is *below* a threshold Δ_θ, indicating insufficient cache size for reads or if average state access latency is *over* a threshold Δ_τ, indicating a significant fraction of operations need costly disk/SSD accesses. In this case, we cancel the scale-out decision (Line 17) and increase the operator's memory level (Line 18). Otherwise, we apply the recommended parallelism.

4.3 Implementation

Justin is implemented in version 1.18 of Apache Flink and extends the Kubernetes Operator [3] where DS2 [17] is implemented. Our changes account for about 1,500 LoC. In addition to the policy described earlier in this section, Justin relies on mechanisms allowing the enactment of the decisions: (1) the support of Task Slots (TS) with heterogeneous memory allocations; (2) the placement of tasks to TS across different Tasks Managers (TMs), minimizing fragmentation, and (3) the creating when necessary of newer TMs.

Flink 1.18 supports an API allowing to specify custom resource configurations for operators when submitting a new query (number of cores and quantity of heap, network, and managed memory). We extend Flink's Adaptive Scheduler module to allow such changes to be enacted at runtime via a REST API. The scheduler maps heterogeneous memory demand to the available TMs using a standard multidimensional Bin-Packing algorithm [20].

The Flink policy is implemented as part of Flink's Kubernetes Operator [3]. An API allows the policy's parameters, such as trigger or decision thresholds, to be dynamically adapted at runtime. This allows control over the elastic scaling of long-running queries without redeployment. When the Bin-Packing algorithm for task placement cannot find enough space with existing TMs, the Kubernetes Operator can spawn a new TM "pod" in the cluster.

5 Evaluation

Our evaluation aims to answer the following research questions:

- For a given target rate, is Justin able to converge to efficient configurations in terms of CPU and memory usage?
- Does the integration of vertical and horizontal scaling lead to a longer convergence time compared to horizontal (i.e., CPU-only) scaling?

---

[1] The algorithm uses strict inequality signs $<$ and $>$ for clarity, but we can use a minimum amount of improvement as a percentage as well, implementing a hysteresis.

We compare Justin and the Flink DS2 implementation and use the obtained rate (i.e., the capacity of a configuration), the sum of assigned CPU cores, and the sum of allocated memory as metrics. We use as workload the standard Nexmark Benchmark [35]. Nexmark simulates an auction system and provides a set of representative queries for the evaluation of batch and stream processing systems.

We use the same six queries as used in the original evaluation of DS2 [17]. All queries use a single source and a single sink operator. Q1 produces currency conversions using one Map operator. Q2 uses a Filter operator to select bids with a specific identifier. Q3 classifies sales based on location and categories and maps them to specific auctions, using an incremental join operator over the complete stream (i.e., without windowing) and two filter operators. Q5 determines the auctions with the most bids in a period and uses one stateful operator and a group-by-aggregate over a sliding window. Q8 monitors new active users over a period and uses a tumbling-windowed join as a stateful operator. Finally, Q11 monitors user sessions by computing the number of bids each user makes while active. It uses one operator, a stateful group-by-aggregate, over a session window.

Experimental Setup. We alternatively deploy Flink with Justin or DS2 on a testbed of 7 nodes, each equipped with two 10-core Intel Xeon E5-2630L v4 CPUs, 128 GB of memory, and a 400 GB SSD. Nodes are connected with 10-Gbps Ethernet. One node hosts the Kubernetes controller, and another hosts Prometheus and Grafana. We deploy the Job Manager on another dedicated node. The four remaining nodes are used to host TMs.

We configure each TM to use 4 CPU cores and 2 GB of memory, shared among 4 TSs. Flink reserves a portion of the available memory for framework management data and JVM-specific data. The default amount of managed memory per TS is 158 MB. With DS2, all tasks get this fixed amount. With Justin vertical scaling, a task may receive from 158 MB ($o_i.m^t = 0$) to 632 MB ($o_i.m^t = 2$, i.e., after two scale-up actions) of managed memory.

We set elastic scaling trigger parameters to keep the average busyness of operators between 20% and 80%. Through experimental analysis, we identify two thresholds that allow suitable identification of memory pressure for some operator's tasks: A cache hit rate over $\Delta_\theta = 80\%$ and an average state access latency over $\Delta_\tau = 1ms$. Similarly to DS2, we use short 2-minute decision windows and a 1-minute stabilization period. If no scaling is triggered at the end of the window, the autoscaler waits for the following full metrics window collection. Metrics are collected and aggregated with a granularity of 5 s.

5.1 Results

Figure 5 presents elastic scaling results for Justin and DS2. We show the achieved rate (capacity) and the resource allocation for the two auto-scalers as a function of time. The objective is for sources to reach the target rate indicated by a thin, dashed blue line after a few reconfigurations. The top plots show the achieved rate, while the bottom plots show the overall CPU and memory consumption (including heap, network, and managed memory). Note that, as in the DS2 paper [17], we exclude sources from the resource count as these are used as

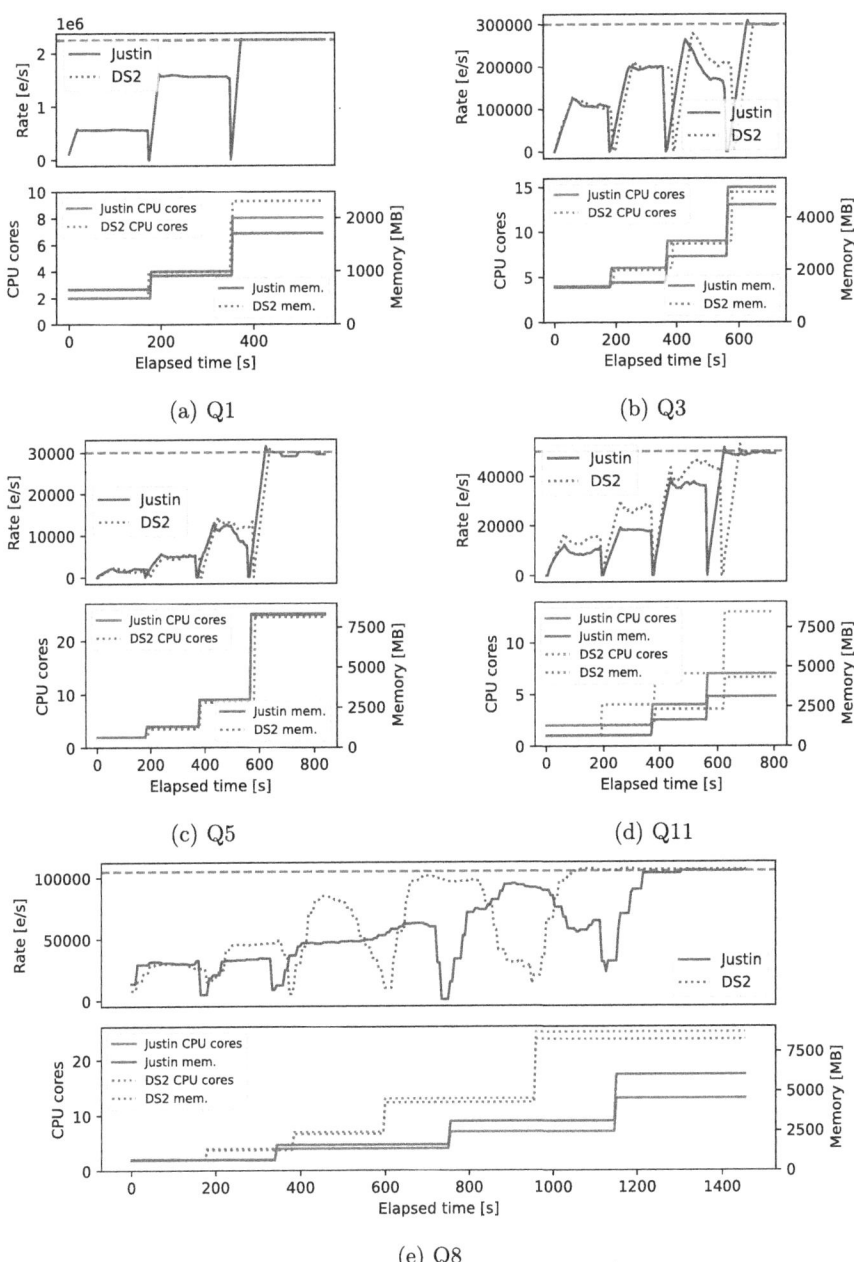

Fig. 5. Elastic scaling performance of Justin (plain lines) compared to DS2 (dotted lines), achieved capacity (purple), and resulting overall CPU cores (red) and memory consumption (green). The horizontal dashed blue line represents the target rate. (Color figure online)

stateless workload injectors that would be replaced by lighter-load Flink sources connected to external sources in production. We include sink operators with a fixed parallelism of one task. Sinks have a low load across all queries and never are a bottleneck.

Q1 and Q2: Stateless, Single-Operator Queries. These two queries feature a single stateless operator. As the results for the two were highly similar, we choose only to show those for Q1. Figure 5a shows that both auto-scalers use two steps to reach a final configuration supporting the 2,250,000 event/s target rate. Both reach a parallelism of 7 tasks for the operator, but Justin disables its managed memory. As a result, the Justin configuration uses 40% less memory, from 2,317 MB for DS2 down to 1,379 MB.

Q3: two Stateless and One Stateful Operator. Q3 performs an unbounded incremental join, but the size of this operator state converges to a relatively small value ($\sim$8 MB), indicating vertical scaling is likely counterproductive. The two other operators are stateless. Figure 5b shows that Justin can free the managed memory of the stateless operators while avoiding unnecessary scale-up for the stateful one, using 10% less memory than DS2. Both auto-scalers converge in the same number of steps. In detail, at the first reconfiguration ($t = 1$, 180 s), stateless operators get configured as $(1; \perp)$ in Justin and $(1; 158)$ in DS2; after two more scaling steps ($t = 3$) the configuration of the stateful operator becomes $(12; 158)$ in both cases.

Q5: Stateful Sliding-Window Aggregation Query. Q5 performs an aggregation over a sliding window, requiring complex access patterns to state in order to re-compute outputs over a new window frequently. Under the Nexmark workload, the state remains small (i.e., $\sim$10 MB). As for Q3, vertical scaling would have no impact on the performance of this query. Justin chooses only to perform horizontal scaling. Yet, it saves a small amount of memory by removing the managed memory of the sink operator, as shown by Fig. 5c. For both auto-scalers, the final configuration for Q5's stateful operator is $(24; 158)$.

We discuss Q11 before Q8 to follow the order of presentation in Fig. 5.

Q11: Stateful Session Window Aggregation Query. Q11 results in Fig. 5d illustrate the benefit of replacing a scale-out decision with a scale-up.

We observe a first reconfiguration a little before 200 s for both auto-scalers. While DS2 increases the parallelism of the primary operator to 3, growing the memory use accordingly, the CPU and memory of Justin remain equal but for a higher resulting capacity. This is explained by the joint decisions of Justin of (1) stripping the sink operator of its unnecessary managed memory and (2) allocating the same amount of memory to the primary operator due to a scale-up decision (i.e., increasing its memory level from 0 to 1 while keeping a single task).

The resulting capacity is lower with Justin but higher when accounted for per expanded core. Follow-up reconfigurations at $\sim$380 s and $\sim$560 s use scale out for both Justin and DS2. However, the better per-task performance of the configuration resulting from the first reconfiguration leads Justin to require 48% lower CPU and a 28% lower memory utilization. The final configuration matching the target rate is (6; 316) for Justin and (12; 158) for DS2. Justin uses the same number of reconfigurations but converges slightly faster than DS2 with this query.

Q8: Stateful Tumbling Window Join. Finally, Fig. 5e presents results for Q8. This query is more complex and requires more reconfigurations to achieve the target rate. As for Q11, the first reconfiguration of DS2 uses a scale-out while Justin triggers a scale-up of the primary stateful operator. Interestingly, and in contrast with q11, the scale-up of Justin seems to have no real benefit, which may lead to thinking one additional round of reconfiguration will be necessary to compensate for a bad decision. The following reconfigurations show the situation is the opposite. Justin performs three scale-out reconfigurations to reach the target rate, while DS2 needs four. We note that Justin intermediate configurations take longer to stabilize than with DS2, resulting in a shorter convergence time for the latter despite the additional step. In terms of resources, however, the advantage is clearly for Justin, with 48% less CPU cores and 27% less memory than DS2 for the same capacity. The primary operator's final configuration is (12; 316) for Justin and (24; 158) for DS2.

Discussion. Our experiments with Nexmark show that Justin exploits hybrid CPU/memory scaling effectively for all queries but one. It saves memory by stripping unnecessary memory from stateless operators (in primary operators of Q1, Q2, and Q3, and for sink operators of all queries). It significantly reduces the overall resource consumption for a given target rate in complex stateful queries (Q8 and Q11), both in terms of memory as expected and, perhaps more unexpectedly, CPU. This latter result is due to the higher efficiency of tasks not constrained by state access that, as a result, do not need to reach high parallelism for the same capacity as constrained ones. Justin results in fewer or the same number of steps as DS2 and comparable convergence time. Finally, we observe that for a query that does not really benefit from hybrid CPU/memory scaling (Q5), Justin does not introduce a penalty over DS2.

6 Related Work

Elastic scaling for stream processing has gathered significant interest over the last decades. Representative works include MEAD [30], hierarchical auto-scaling [31], DS2 [17], and more [8,15,34]. Surveys by Röger and Mayer [28] and Cardellini *et al.* [10] provide a comprehensive analysis of this field. To the best of our knowledge, no elastic scaling method combining dynamic memory allocation with horizontal scaling has been proposed by previous work on the topic.

Resource management in distributed stream processing has also attracted significant interest. A survey by Liu *et al.* [19] presents an overview of the topic. Integrating state management with stream processing operators led to advances in programmability and fault tolerance [5,9,22]. StreamBed [29] uses interpolation techniques from guided small-scale runs to build a model and predict resource consumption, including CPU and memory, for large-scale Flink instances. Recently, Wang *et al.* [37] proposed CAPSys, a new algorithm for assigning task slots to tasks in Flink that takes into account colocation effects between tasks and competition for resources such as memory and I/O. CAPSys reduces the unpredictability of round-robin or random task-to-TM assignments. Adapting its approach to the placement problem in Justin, where tasks have different memory granularity, is undoubtedly an interesting perspective of our work.

Understanding the performance of LSM-based storage [21,25], including its relation to available memory, is a complex problem. Gadget [7] is a benchmark of backend storage operations in a DSP, targeting Flink and RocksDB. Tutorials by Sarkar *et al.* [32,33] are a good source of references on optimizations for LSM-based stores and optimization of read operations.

Memory management and allocation is an important topic in non-stream (i.e., batch) processing systems. MespaConfig [39] optimizes the memory configuration of *multiple* Spark batch processing jobs co-located on a cluster. Iorgulescu *et al.* [16] define the memory elasticity principle and show how careful memory allocation below the working set size of batch processing, in-memory applications can yield close performance to larger allocations and implement resulting scheduling policies in Apache Yarn. The specificities of write-optimized, LSM-based storage in RocksDB prevent from directly applying these techniques.

Finally, we note that the idea of combining horizontal and vertical scaling in a hybrid auto-scaler has been explored in other contexts, such as cloud workloads, e.g., with HoloScale [23], or for serving model inference [27].

7 Conclusion

We presented Justin, a hybrid CPU and memory auto-scaler for Apache Flink. In contrast with DS2, Flink current auto-scaler integrated with its Kubernetes operator, Justin arbitrates between horizontal scaling and vertical scaling based on metrics from the RocksDB storage layer. Results on the classical Nexmark benchmark show that Justin can achieve similar capacity as DS2 when reconfiguring towards a target rate while using fewer resources.

This work opens several interesting perspectives. First, and similarly to DS2, Justin makes implicit assumptions about the absence of skew, i.e., unbalanced key popularities leading to an imbalanced load between the different tasks of an operator. A solution to this problem is explicitly rebalancing keys between tasks instead of using only a hash function [13,24]. This does not address the fact that, in some cases, popular keys may be associated with a more significant state. In this case, heterogeneous memory allocation between tasks of the same operator could be an option, although it would require a significantly more complex auto-scaler. Second, a complementary path to Justin reactive auto-scaling approach would be to predict operators' response to memory availability, either by allowing programmers to provide hints or by running them in isolation and modeling their performance [6]. Finally, Justin and DS2 consider the auto-scaling and resource allocation of queries in isolation. An auto-scaler that considers the co-placement of query tasks, e.g., running memory-intensive tasks of some queries with stateless tasks of another query, may lead to better consolidation and platform resource use overall.

Acknowledgments. This research was funded by the Walloon region (Belgium) through the Win2Wal project "GEPICIAD" and by a gift from Eura Nova. Experiments presented in this paper were carried out using the Grid'5000 testbed, supported by a scientific interest group hosted by Inria and including CNRS, RENATER and several Universities as well as other organizations (see https://www.grid5000.fr).

References

1. Apache flink (2025). https://flink.apache.org/
2. Apache storm (2025). https://storm.apache.org/
3. Flink kubernetes operator (2025). https://github.com/apache/flink-kubernetes-operator
4. Rocksdb (2025). https://rocksdb.org/
5. Affetti, L., Margara, A., Cugola, G.: Flowdb: integrating stream processing and consistent state management. In: DEBS 2017, pp. 134–145 (2025)
6. Agnihotri, P., Koldehofe, B., Stiegele, P., Heinrich, R., Binnig, C., Luthra, M.: Zerotune: learned zero-shot cost models for parallelism tuning in stream processing. In: ICDE 2024 (2024)
7. Asyabi, E., Wang, Y., Liagouris, J., Kalavri, V., Bestavros, A.: A new benchmark harness for systematic and robust evaluation of streaming state stores. In: EuroSys 2022 (2022)
8. Barazzutti, R., et al.: Elastic scaling of a high-throughput content-based publish/subscribe engine. In: ICDCS 2014, pp. 567–576 (2014)
9. Carbone, P., Ewen, S., Fóra, G., Haridi, S., Richter, S., Tzoumas, K.: State management in apache flink®: consistent stateful distributed stream processing. Proc. VLDB Endow. **10**(12), 1718–1729 (2017)
10. Cardellini, V., Lo Presti, F., Nardelli, M., Russo, G.: Runtime adaptation of data stream processing systems: the state of the art. ACM Comput. Surv. **54**(11s), 1–36 (2022)
11. CNCF: Prometheus (2024). https://prometheus.io/
12. Dong, S., Kryczka, A., Jin, Y., Stumm, M.: RocksDB: evolution of development priorities in a key-value store serving large-scale applications. ACM Trans. Storage **17**(4) (2021)
13. Fang, J., Zhang, R., Fu, T.Z., Zhang, Z., Zhou, A., Zhu, J.: Parallel stream processing against workload skewness and variance. In: ACM HPDC 2017 (2017)
14. Fragkoulis, M., Carbone, P., Kalavri, V., Katsifodimos, A.: A survey on the evolution of stream processing systems. VLDB J. **33**(2), 507–541 (2024)
15. Gedik, B., Schneider, S., Hirzel, M., Wu, K.L.: Elastic scaling for data stream processing. TPDS **25**(6), 1447–1463 (2013)
16. Iorgulescu, C., Dinu, F., Raza, A., Hassan, W.U., Zwaenepoel, W.: Don't cry over spilled records: memory elasticity of data-parallel applications and its application to cluster scheduling. In: USENIX ATC 2017, pp. 97–109 (2017)
17. Kalavri, V., Liagouris, J., Hoffmann, M., Dimitrova, D., Forshaw, M., Roscoe, T.: Three steps is all you need: fast, accurate, automatic scaling decisions for distributed streaming dataflows. In: OSDI 2018 (2018)

18. Kreps, J., Narkhede, N., Rao, J., et al.: Kafka: a distributed messaging system for log processing. In: Proceedings of the NetDB, vol. 11 (2011)
19. Liu, X., Buyya, R.: Resource management and scheduling in distributed stream processing systems: a taxonomy, review, and future directions. ACM Comput. Surv. (CSUR) **53**(3), 1–41 (2020)
20. Lodi, A., Martello, S., Vigo, D.: Recent advances on two-dimensional bin packing problems. Disc. Appl. Math. **123**(1–3), 379–396 (2002)
21. Luo, C., Carey, M.J.: Lsm-based storage techniques: a survey. VLDB J. **29**(1), 393–418 (2020)
22. Madsen, K.G.S., Zhou, Y.: Dynamic resource management in a massively parallel stream processing engine. In: CIKM 2025, pp. 13–22 (2025)
23. Millnert, V., Eker, J.: Holoscale: horizontal and vertical scaling of cloud resources. In: UCC 2020, pp. 196–205 (2020)
24. Nasir, M.A.U., Morales, G.D.F., Kourtellis, N., Serafini, M.: When two choices are not enough: balancing at scale in distributed stream processing. In: ICDE 2016, pp. 589–600 (2016)
25. O'Neil, P., Cheng, E., Gawlick, D., O'Neil, E.: The log-structured merge-tree (lsm-tree). Acta Informatica **33**, 351–385 (1996)
26. Rabl, T., Traub, J., Katsifodimos, A., Markl, V.: Apache flink in current research. IT-Inf. Tech. **58**(4) (2016)
27. Razavi, K., Salmani, M., Mühlhäuser, M., Koldehofe, B., Wang, L.: A tale of two scales: reconciling horizontal and vertical scaling for inference serving systems. arXiv preprint arXiv:2407.14843 (2024)
28. Röger, H., Mayer, R.: A comprehensive survey on parallelization and elasticity in stream processing. ACM Comput. Surv. **52**(2), 1–37 (2019)
29. Rosinosky, G., Schmitz, D., Rivière, E.: Streambed: capacity planning for stream processing. In: DEBS 2024, pp. 90–102 (2024)
30. Russo, G.R., Cardellini, V., Casale, G., Presti, F.L.: MEAD: model-based vertical auto-scaling for data stream processing. In: CCGrid 2021, pp. 314–323 (2025)
31. Russo Russo, G., Cardellini, V., Lo Presti, F.: Hierarchical auto-scaling policies for data stream processing on heterogeneous resources. ACM Trans. Auton. Adapt. Syst. (2023)
32. Sarkar, S., Athanassoulis, M.: Dissecting, designing, and optimizing LSM-based data stores. In: SIGMOD 2022, pp. 2489–2497 (2022)
33. Sarkar, S., Dayan, N., Athanassoulis, M.: The LSM design space and its read optimizations. In: ICDE 2023, pp. 3578–3584. IEEE (2023)
34. Schneider, S., Andrade, H., Gedik, B., Biem, A., Wu, K.L.: Elastic scaling of data parallel operators in stream processing. In: IPDPS 2009, pp. 1–12 (2009)
35. Tucker, P., Tufte, K., Papadimos, V., Maier, D.: Nexmark–a benchmark for queries over data streams (draft). Technical report (2008)
36. Verwiebe, J., Grulich, P.M., Traub, J., Markl, V.: Survey of window types for aggregation in stream processing systems. VLDB J., 1–27 (2023)
37. Wang, Y., Huang, L., Wang, Z., Kalavri, V., Matta, I.: CAPSys: contention-aware task placement for data stream processing. In: EuroSys 2025 (2025)
38. Zaharia, M., Das, T., Li, H., Hunter, T., Shenker, S., Stoica, I.: Discretized streams: fault-tolerant streaming computation at scale. In: SOSP 2013 (2013)
39. Zong, Z., Wen, L., Hu, X., Han, R., Qian, C., Lin, L.: Mespaconfig: memory-sparing configuration auto-tuning for co-located in-memory cluster computing jobs. IEEE Trans. Serv. Comput. **15**(5), 2883–2896 (2021)

AIõRT: AI-Driven Distributed System for Heterogenous Internet of Robotic Things in Sustainable Ecosystem

Hanyue Xu[1,2], Yuanxin Su[1,2], Kah Phooi Seng[3(✉)], Chenghao Li[1], Han Lu[1], Jianfei He[1], and Li-Minn Ang[3]

[1] Xi'an Jiaotong-Liverpool University, Suzhou, China
hanyue.xu19@student.xjtlu.edu.cn
[2] University of Liverpool, Liverpool, UK
[3] University of the Sunshine Coast, Petrie, QLD 4502, Australia
jseng@usc.edu.au

Abstract. The convergence of Artificial Intelligence (AI) and the Internet of Things (IoT) has paved the way for the Internet of Robotic Things (IoRT), where autonomous robotic systems leverage AI capabilities to operate seamlessly in interconnected ecosystems. However, traditional IoRT architectures reliant on cloud computing face critical challenges, including data privacy risks, latency, and bandwidth limitations. This paper proposes a novel AI-driven distributed system, AI õ RT, that utilizes edge computing to distribute computational resources closer to robotic devices, enabling reduced response times and enhanced data security. The system employs layered architecture integrating edge AI, heterogeneous edge-split federated learning, and FPGA-accelerated binary compressive sensing (BinCSNet) for efficient model training and data processing. This design optimizes resource usage, supports real-time decision-making, and facilitates scalable deployment across heterogeneous networks. The system also demonstrated its scalability at the robot service level through humanoid robot-based application cases, gait emotion recognition and human depression detection, highlighting its potential to advance autonomous systems in sustainable and secure environments.

Keywords: Artificial Intelligence of Things (AIoT) · Edge computing · Distributed learning · compressive sensing

1 Introduction

Recently, many Internet of Robotic Things (IoRT) systems have been proposed in the literature based on cloud computing, called "Cloud robot" [1]. In this paradigm, robots are not only equipped with sensors and basic processing units but also connect to cloud platforms that provide extensive computational resources, data storage, and advanced AI algorithms. Although, cloud computing brings benefits to the IoRT system, it suffers from various issues such as data privacy, latency, and bandwidth limitations. The advent of edge computing and advancements in edge AI hardware provide a compelling alternative by relocating computational tasks closer to devices, reducing dependence on centralized infrastructure. Moreover, distributed and decentralized learning frameworks, such as federated learning [2] and split learning [3], enable collaborative model training across devices without compromising data privacy. These technologies enhance system scalability and privacy, but struggle to deal with a heterogeneous network of systems with mobile devices.

However, the heterogeneity of devices is limited real-time performance and resource allocation, especially for high-dimensional data. Compressive sensing (CS) offers efficient sparse data representation [4], but traditional CS methods struggle with heterogeneous, resource-constrained IoRT systems. These challenges can be addressed by redesigning system architecture and deploying lightweight, optimized algorithms.

To improve the efficiency of distributed learning and data processing in IoRT heterogeneous system, we propose AIõRT distributed system, and edge-based AI-driven distributed system that can be used in a sustainable ecosystem. By leveraging perception, edge computing, and distributed intelligence, robots are enabled to make autonomous decisions and interact with intelligent environments in real time. We improved the hierarchical architecture of the original IoRT and added the concept of AI intelligent nodes, so that the system can be easily extended to the autonomous decision-making of AI-powered robots in complex environments. For the heterogeneous network of IoRT system, a heterogeneous edge-split federated learning framework and a lightweight BinCSNet compressed sensing algorithm are proposed, which can improve the efficiency of distributed edge learning while protecting data privacy, and provide edge computing performance to reduce the consumption of hardware resources. The major contributions of this research work are as follows: a): Proposed a heterogeneous edge-split federated learning framework and a distributed aggregation strategy based on cloud edge collaboration to balance the computing resources of edge devices, protect data privacy, and improve the learning efficiency of distributed AI models. b): Designed with FPGA-based computing units, this algorithm supports heterogeneous computing with highly flexible parallel control. It enables simultaneous communication and data processing alongside CPUs, enhancing overall data processing efficiency and conserving hardware resources.

2 Proposed Hierarchical Architecture of AIõRT

The traditional IoRT architecture depends on cloud computing for storage and processing to serve mobile robots. However, this centralized structure results in inefficient data transmission, resource allocation, and privacy concerns. Thus, there is a need to shift toward distributed IoRT architectures. This section introduces an AI-driven hierarchical architecture based on distributed learning for the AI õ RT distributed system, comprising the physical sensor layer, robot & mobile device layer, edge intelligence layer, cloud intelligence layer, and applications & services layer, as shown in Fig. 1.

The Physical Sensor Layer. The physical sensor layer includes various IoT sensors and robot sensor components, monitoring critical environmental parameters, energy usage, and intelligent environment perception [5]. Robots act as intelligent agents interacting with sensors to collaboratively execute tasks.

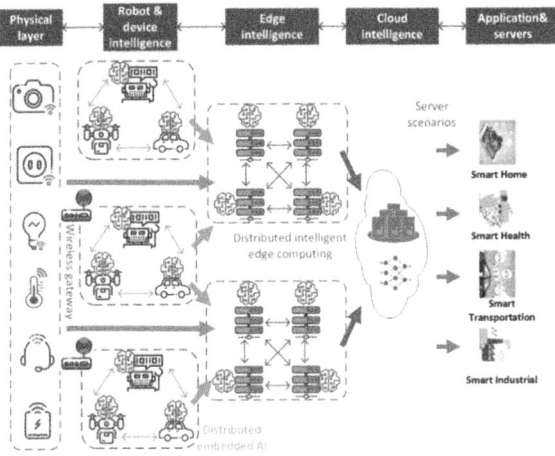

Fig. 1. The proposed hierarchical architecture of AIðRT distributed system

The Robot and Mobile Devices Intelligence Layer. The robot & mobile device intelligence layer is the core intelligence of the AIðRT system, containing robots, intelligent vehicles, drones, and mobile agents. Equipped with embedded AI processors for computing and storage, these devices handle real-time perception, decision-making, control, communication, and human-robot interaction (HRI) tasks. Through AI, they actively learn from physical sensor data and coordinate with other devices via decentralized learning [6]. This layer ensures that robots and IoT devices are not just passive data collectors, but active agents capable of making real-time decisions and autonomous operations. Devices can perform complex tasks by offloading data to edge intelligence through wireless networks or by partially outsourcing neural network operations to edge resources when their capacities are limited [7].

The Edge Intelligence Layer. The edge intelligence layer is usually composed of wireless base stations, routers, and IoT gateways close to intelligent robot devices, which can provide certain computing and storage capabilities. This layer aims to make full use of the resources of intelligent edge servers to achieve complex AI model training through distributed learning networks, to reduce the dependence on cloud resources which leads to communication delays of the system. Through technologies such as federated learning and peer-to-peer knowledge sharing [8], devices collaborate to train models by sharing model updates rather than raw data, thereby protecting data privacy and minimizing bandwidth usage. This decentralized approach allows for continuous, incremental learning as each robot device adapts to new data and environmental changes in real time, ensuring robust and context-aware AI performance.

Network edge nodes provide network connectivity to other edge nodes, robotic devices, and sensors to integrate a stable system, reducing the possibility of a single point of failure. There are several main communication protocols, depending on the distance the physical layer sends data, and the power required. IEEE 802.15.4 (WiFi) and Bluetooth are common short-range protocols, while common remote protocols are

LoRaWAN and NB-IoT [9]. The low-rate protocol is especially suitable for small battery-powered robots or IoT sensing components due to its low power consumption and low cost. Therefore, it is the focus of AIõRT system to realize low-rate wireless network transmission of sensors and actuators in the physical layer.

The Cloud Intelligence Layer. The cloud intelligence layer comprises high-performance computing centers supporting the edge and robot intelligence layers with advanced intelligent decisions. It primarily manages task offloading and scheduling [10], aggregates local models from the edge layer, and optimizes communication resources, improving the overall system performance.

The Applications and Services Layer. The application & server layer is the development layer of the architecture and focuses on exploring specific services and applications that can be delivered to users through robots. By integrating and analyzing sensor and device data, this layer supports intelligent automation, enabling robots to dynamically adapt to varying conditions and fulfill diverse industrial needs.

3 Design of Distributed System AIõRT

Figure 2 illustrates an AI-driven distributed system, AI õ RT designed for heterogeneous IoRT networks within the new hierarchical architecture. The system introduces AI intelligent nodes near autonomous robots, enhancing data processing speed and reducing transmission times. It comprises sensors, interconnected edge devices (edge nodes, AI intelligent nodes), cloud servers, and mobile robots. Utilizing cloud-edge collaborative learning, it decreases energy consumption and boosts robotic autonomous intelligence. Data from dynamic environments is distributed based on complexity, facilitating global AI model training. The system optimizes data transmission for hardware efficiency through a binary compressed sensing depth model, allowing hardware flexibility. This section covers distributed edge computing, data transfer modules, HRI capabilities, and their interplay within the AIõRT distributed system.

3.1 Edge-Cloud Collaborative Distributed Learning for AIõRT

Robot autonomous intelligence depends significantly on data processing and learning capabilities of the AIõRT system. At the edge intelligence layer, we propose a distributed learning framework incorporating cloud-edge collaboration and heterogeneous edge-split federated learning (Fig. 3) to balance edge computing resource heterogeneity and improve distributed model training efficiency.

Heterogeneous Edge-Split Federated Learning. Federated learning preserves privacy by sharing only local model parameters, constructing a global model through aggregation. Given the diverse computational capabilities of IoRT edge devices (high-performance AI intelligent nodes and less powerful IoT sensor gateways), we introduce a cloud-edge split learning framework built on federated learning. By partitioning local neural networks w, computational loads are redistributed to more powerful edge nodes. The local neural network of sensor gateways (edge) is split into subnetworks w^I (input

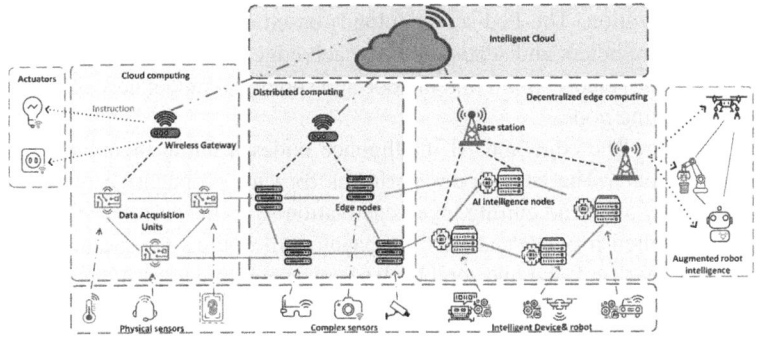

Fig. 2. The proposed overall architecture of AI-Driven sensing AIðRT system for HRI

layer on IoT edge devices) and w^O (output layer on AI intelligent nodes), with complete networks retained on higher-performance AI nodes. Leveraging parallel processing, AI intelligent nodes handle forward-propagated intermediate (smash) data from w^I and execute forward and back-propagation on w^O to calculate gradients for w^I.

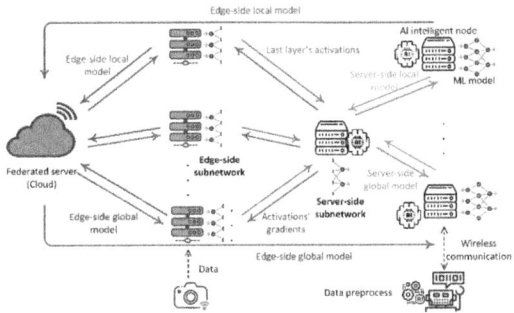

Fig. 3. Illustration of heterogeneous edge-split federated learning

Cloud-Edge Collaborative Aggregation Strategy. AI intelligent nodes, equipped with substantial computing and storage resources and positioned near mobile robots, deploy complete AI models. To engage every node in optimizing the global model, we developed a cloud-edge collaborative aggregation algorithm that integrates distributed learning models derived from IoT sensor and robot data. The aggregation algorithm aims to identify a global model minimizing the overall loss function $\mathcal{L}(W)$ through the aggregation of local models w_i, formulated as [11]:

$$F(W) = \frac{\sum_{i=1}[s_i]f_i(w) + \sum_{j=1}[d_j]f_j(w)}{[D]}, i \in K, j \in N, \quad (1)$$

where $[\cdot]$ is the number of element, K and N are the set of IoT edge nodes and AI intelligence nodes. D is overall data, where $s, d \in D$. The step of this algorithm in t iteration are follows:

(a) Model initialization. The Fed server (cloud) based on learning task initializes the ML model parameters and sends them to each edge node and AI intelligent node. Each edge node selects AI intelligent node and split local model network and offload to corresponding nodes.
(b) Local training. The edge and AI intelligence nodes training their local model by local sensor data. The edge nodes performs forward propagation on subnetwork $f(s, w^I) \to A_t$ and send cutting layer's activation A_t to the selected AI intelligence node, which then forward and back propagates till obtains the gradient of cutting layer $dA_t := \nabla \mathcal{L}(w^O; A_t)$ and send back to corresponding edge node.
(c) Gradient aggregation. The k edge nodes upload the received gradient of w_k^I to Fed server and AI intelligence nodes upload the gradient of subnetwork w_n^I in complete model to Fed server. Then, server aggregate all gradient $\nabla W_t^I \leftarrow \sum_{i=1}^{K} \nabla w_i^I + \sum_{i=1}^{N} \nabla w_j^I$ and average. Same operation for subnetwork w^O in AI intelligence node.
(d) *Model update.* Each AI intelligent node and edge nodes updates the local model through the global gradient of the Fed server and the offloaded AI intelligent node $W_{n,(t+1)} = W_{n,t} - \eta \frac{d_j}{D}(\nabla W_t^I + \nabla W_t^O)$ and begin the next round training.

3.2 Embedded AI for IoT Edge Nodes

The hardware resources of IoT nodes often cannot support full-precision DNNs. Binary Neural Networks (BNNs) are considered an extreme form of quantized models, mapping full-precision data to binary values $\{-1, 1\}$ [12]. This reduces the number of bits needed for data storage and significantly lowers the computational resources required. The quantization rule can be expressed as:

$$sign(x) = \begin{cases} -1, & \text{if } x \leq 0 \\ 1, & \text{if } x > 0 \end{cases} \quad (2)$$

Additionally, matrix multiplication can also be replaced by:

$$X * W \approx sign(X) \circledast sign(W) = X_b \circledast W_b \quad (3)$$

where W and X denotes weights of convolutional layer and input. X_b and W_b denotes the binarized inputs and weights respectively. $\circledast$ denotes the XNOR-pop count operation.

Along with the standard binarization process, we introduced the scaling factor as a learnable parameter to enhance the representation of binarized weights and activations. By using inner products, we combined the scaling factors for weights and activations into one matrix. Thus, during inference, the scaling factor matrix only needs to perform element-wise multiplication with the convolution layer output, removing the need for resource-heavy matrix inner product multiplication. The process can be described as:

$$X * W \approx (X_b \circledast W_b) \odot (\alpha \otimes \beta) = (X_b \circledast W_b) \odot \Gamma \quad (4)$$

where α and β are scaling factor of weights and activation. $\odot$ represents the matrix multiplication (inner product).

Consequently, based on CSNet [13], and the aforementioned theories, we proposed the BinCSNet, consisting of three parts: sampling, initial reconstruction, and deep reconstruction. The sampling is responsible for compressing the image into its corresponding sparse representation, which can then be efficiently transmitted between nodes. At the receiver, the model's reconstruction is needed to rebuild the image. In the initial reconstruction, we retain full-precision weights to ensure minimal information loss. Subsequently, binary deep reconstruction blocks further refine the image details, enhancing the detail representation of the image.

4 Applications of the Proposed AIõRT Distributed System

To further indicate the feasibility of our AIõRT distributed system in the real world, we integrate the AIõRT with two HRI systems, Human-Robot Depression Detection System and Human-Robot Pose Imitation System. The implementation of these two systems following steps: i) Data logging and initial processing (AI Intelligent Node): Lightweight BinCSNet compressed sensing algorithms are used to optimize data transfer and reduce the computation-intensive on-board hard ware of the robot. ii): Distributed learning: Heterogeneous edge-split federated learning is applied to train the machine learning models with different data sources to improve representative feature extraction while maintaining data privacy. iii) Model inferencing and Robot responding: the trained models transmit the predict results to the robot, who responses to human depending on these results.

In human-robot depression detection system, the robot initiates a brief interview with the user. Audio features are extracted from the user's speech using methods described in [14], and a classifier subsequently predicts the presence or absence of depression. Based on the prediction, the robot verbally communicates the diagnostic result to the user. In human-robot imitation system, the robot captures an image of the user, where skeletal data—comprising joint coordinates—are extracted and reconstructed by the machine learning approach proposed in [15]. Based on the reconstructed skeleton, the robot imitates the pose of the user.

5 Experiments

5.1 Evaluation of Edge Distributed Learning in AIõRT System

Experiment Setup. Based on Docker 24.0.7 and TCP socket API 1.43, the experiment uses isolated containers in Docker to simulate the edge gateway node and AI intelligent node of the edge layer and cloud server for AIõRT system. All programs are written by Python3.6 and Pytorch 1.11.0 and built on a desktop computer (NVIDIA GeForce RTX4080 GPU and Intel Core i9-12900K CPU). We also use Secure Sockets Layer (SSL) to encrypt parameters when they are uploaded and used MQTT protocol for cloud-edge communication. We utilized two deep learning models ResNet18 and AlexNet and two public datasets HAM10000 and MNIST to verify the performance of heterogeneous edge-split federated learning frameworks. In the distributed training phase, the batch size for HAM10000 and MNIST are 1024 and 32 respectively. Both datasets are divided into training set, validation set and test set with the ratios 8:1:1. For each model, model Splitting was implemented at the third layer (Batch Normalization) in ResNet18 and the second layer (Maxpool) in AlexNet.

Table 1. Test Results for distributed training

Dataset	Models	Centr	FL	SFL	Ours
HAM10000	ResNet18	79.2%	77.5%	79.0%	78.8%
HAM10000	AlexNet	79.8%	75.0%	70.5%	75.5%
MNIST	ResNet18	99.4%	99.2%	99.0%	99.1%
MNIST	AlexNet	99.1%	98.9%	96.9%	97.8%

Performance of Heterogeneous Edge-Splitting Federated Learning. We use the results of centralized learning as a benchmark to test the performance of proposed algorithm. Table 1 summarizes the test results for 30 global epochs. In the experiment, five nodes and one cloud node were deployed in the federation Learning (FL), splitfed learning (SFL) [16] and proposed algorithm, respectively. The nodes in AIõRT system is composed of two edge nodes and three AI intelligent nodes. In addition, the test accuracy is the average in each global epoch.

As shown in Table 1, heterogeneous edge-split federated learning performs well in experimental settings, with no significant differences between centralized and federated learning. We observed that our algorithm showed better learning performance on large deep learning models (ResNet18), which due to the AI intelligent nodes learning the complete model at each global epoch and aggregating it with the sub-network of the edge nodes. We randomly selected an edge node and recorded its accuracy and loss in each global epoch, as shown in Fig. 4 (a) The loss of our algorithm starts at about 1.4 and steadily decreases, converges after approximately 10 epochs. In contrast, the convergence time of FL begins to stabilize after about 18 global epochs. With similar precision, our algorithm has faster convergence efficiency in distributed learning at the edge layer.

Communication Measurement. We tested the data traffic of four distributed algorithm- FL. SFL, Split learning (SL) in AIõRT setting. Figure 4 (b) shows the average data upload volume for ResNet18 on HAM10000 in each global epoch under 5 and 20 nodes (AIõRT sets 12 edge nodes and 8 AI intelligence nodes). When there are fewer edge nodes, our algorithm uploads more on large datasets because edge nodes need to transmit smash data to AI intelligent nodes. However, the amount of data we upload in AIõRT is mainly focused on communication between edge networks and is much less than the amount of data FL uploads to the cloud, which is about 20% lower. In fact, our algorithm has a lower latency. It is worth noting that the data upload volume of our algorithm is significantly smaller than that of SL and SFL, because the aggregation between AI intelligent nodes depends only on the size of the model parameters. Therefore, our distributed algorithm reduces communication energy consumption while maintaining stable accuracy in AIõRT system.

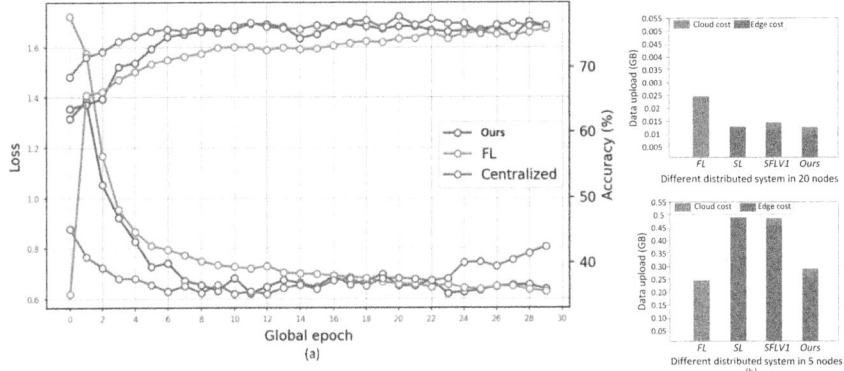

Fig. 4 Test loss and convergence of ResNet18 on HAM10000 (a), Average data upload per global epoch for ResNet18 on HAM10000 (b).

5.2 Evaluation of BinCSNet

We conducted a hardware analysis of BinCSNet to visually demonstrate the differences in computational and memory resources between the binarized network and the full-precision model. In our experiments, the experimental platforms are based on two development boards: Z7P and PYNQ-Z2. Z7P is a development board that uses Xilinx components from the same series as ZCU104 (xczu7ev-ffvc1156-2-i). The Xilinx component for PYNQ-Z2 is XC7Z020CLG400-1. Our model is trained on BSD500 datasets that contain 200 training image and 200 test images [17]. The results are shown in the Table 2, where BOPs (Bit Operations) represent the bit-level operations used to quantify the computational cost or workload, especially in hardware implementations.

Table 2. Comparison of inference hardware cost

Parts	Ratio	Precision	BOPs ($\times 10^7$)	layer outputs (bits)	layer parameters ($\times 10^5$ bits)
Sampling	0.1	Bin	3.008	29376	1.044
		Full-precision	96.259	29376	33.423
	0.3	Bin	9.0538	88416	3.144
		Full-precision	289.722	88416	100.598
Reconstruction	-	Bin	399.778	22.679	15.699
	-	Full-precision	3861.847	22.679	130.949

5.3 Application of AIõRT System with the NAO Robot

In our research, the NAO robot is employed to execute predefined responses in two HRI systems, human-robot depression detection system and human-robot pose imitation system. Standing 57.4 cm tall and weighing 5.4 kg, NAO is designed with 25 degrees of freedom, which enables a wide range of motion. Additionally, the robot is equipped with cameras, ultrasonic and touch sensors, as well as an inertial measurement unit to facilitate environmental perception. For human-robot interaction, it is also integrated with microphones and speakers. Figure 5 illustrates the processes of the human-robot pose imitation system. The NAO robot captures the image of the user's pose and sends it to the AIõRT, where skeletal data is reconstructed and transferred to the parameters for controlling positions and angles of the NAO robot's joints, achieving the human robot imitation.

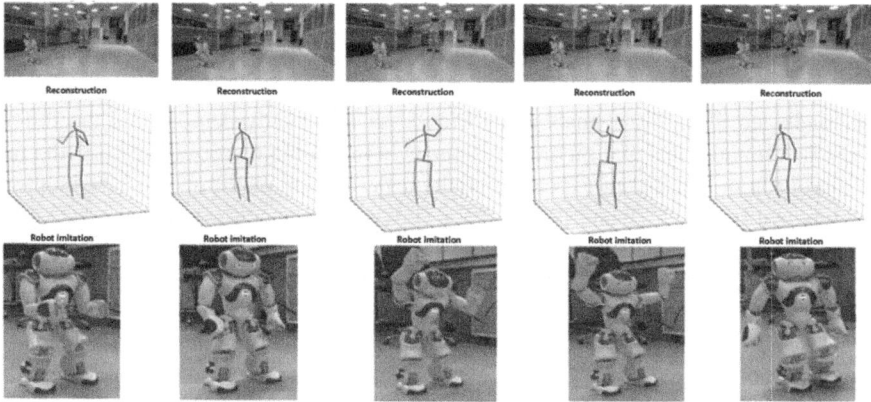

Fig. 5 Real Process of NAO human-robot pose imitation system

6 Conclusion

In this paper, we proposed a novel distributed-based hierarchical architecture for the Internet of Robotic Things (IoRT) and designed an AI-driven AIõRT distributed system tailored to this framework. By integrating edge computing with distributed intelligence, the system empowers robots with enhanced autonomy for mobile devices while achieving energy efficiency. We introduced BinCSNet, a lightweight compressed sensing algorithm coupled with FPGA-based computational units, to optimize data transmission and processing, effectively conserving hardware resources and improving system efficiency. The proposed system is validated through real-world applications, including mental health monitoring tasks such as gait emotion recognition and depression detection. These applications demonstrate the system's versatility, scalability, and potential to facilitate intelligent, sustainable, and low-energy human-computer interactions in complex environments.

References

1. Ray, P.P.: Internet of robotic things: concept, technologies, and challenges. IEEE Access **4**, 9489–9500 (2016)
2. Wang, S., et al.: Adaptive federated learning in resource constrained edge computing systems. IEEE J. Sel. Areas Commun. **37**(6), 1205–1221 (2019)
3. Lyu, X., Liu, S., Liu, J., Ren, C.: Scalable aggregated split learning for data-driven edge intelligence on internet-of-things. IEEE Internet of Things Mag. **6**(4), 124–129 (2023)
4. Amini, A., Marvasti, F.: Deterministic construction of binary, bipolar, and ternary compressed sensing matrices. IEEE Trans. Inf. Theory **57**(4), 2360–2370 (2011)
5. Alammari, A., Moiz, S.A., Negi, A.: Enhanced layered fog architecture for IoT sensing and actuation as a service. Sci. Rep. **11**(1), 21693 (2021)
6. Barbieri, L., Savazzi, S., Brambilla, M., Nicoli, M.: Decentralized federated learning for extended sensing in 6G connected vehicles. Veh. Commun. **33**, 100396 (2022)
7. Chen, Y., Sun, Y., Hao, Y., Taleb, T.: Joint task and computing resource allocation in distributed edge computing systems via multi-agent deep reinforcement learning. IEEE Trans. Netw. Sci. Eng. **11**(4), 3479–3494 (2024). https://doi.org/10.1109/TNSE.2024.3375374
8. Lin, Y., Wang, X., Ma, H., Wang, L., Hao, F., Cai, Z.: An efficient approach to sharing edge knowledge in 5G-enabled industrial Internet of Things. IEEE Trans. Industr. Inf. **19**(1), 930–939 (2022)
9. Peng, H.: WIFI network information security analysis research. In: 2nd International Conference on Consumer Electronics, Communications and Networks (CECNet), pp. 2243–2245. IEEE (2012)
10. Zeng, T., et al.: An offline-transfer-online framework for cloud-edge collaborative distributed reinforcement learning. IEEE Trans. Parallel Distrib. Syst. **35**(5), 720–731 (2024). https://doi.org/10.1109/TPDS.2024.3360438
11. Liang, Z., Yang, P., Zhang, C., Lyu, X.: Secure and efficient hierarchical decentralized learning for internet of vehicles. IEEE Open J. Commun. Soc. **4**, 1417–1429 (2023). https://doi.org/10.1109/OJCOMS.2023.3290625
12. Bulat, A., Tzimiropoulos, G.: Xnor-net++: improved binary neural networks. arXiv preprint arXiv:1909.13863 (2019)
13. Shi, W., Jiang, F., Liu, S., Zhao, D.: Image compressed sensing using convolutional neural network. IEEE Trans. Image Process. **29**, 375–388 (2019)
14. Cho, K., et al.: Learning phrase representations using RNN encoder-decoder for statistical machine translation. arXiv preprint arXiv:1406.1078 (2014)
15. Li, C., Seng, K.P., Ang, L.M.: Gait-to-gait emotional human-robot interaction utilizing trajectories-aware and skeleton-graph-aware spatial-temporal transformer. Sensors (Basel, Switzerland) **25**(3), 734 (2025)
16. Thapa, C., Arachchige, P.C.M., Camtepe, S., Sun, L.: Splitfed: when federated learning meets split learning. Proc. AAAI Conf. Artif. Intell. **36**(8), 8485–8493 (2022)
17. Arbelaez, P., Maire, M., Fowlkes, C., Malik, J.: Contour detection and hierarchical image segmentation. IEEE Trans. Pattern Anal. Mach. Intell. **33**(5), 898–916 (2010)

Author Index

A
Ang, Li-Minn   119
Aublin, Pierre-Louis   43

C
Crumeyrolle, Suzanne   84

D
Desauw, Lauric   1

F
Ferreira, Paulo   64

H
He, Jianfei   119

J
Jonglez, Baptiste   25

K
Kaddour, Sidi Mohammed   25

L
Li, Chenghao   119
Lu, Han   119
Luxey-Bitri, Adrien   1

M
Martiny, Nadège   84

P
Philippe, Jolan   25

R
Raes, Rémy   1
Rahmani, Maryam   84
Rivière, Etienne   102
Rosinosky, Guillaume   102
Rouvoy, Romain   1, 84
Ruas, Olivier   1
Rudametkin, Walter   1

S
Schmitz, Donatien   102
Seng, Kah Phooi   119
Simonin, Matthieu   25
Su, Yuanxin   119

V
Veiga, Luís   64
Vijouyeh, Lyla Naghipour   64
Vogel, Arne   43

X
Xu, Hanyue   119

The manufacturer's authorised representative in the EU is Springer Nature Customer Service Centre GmbH, Europaplatz 3, 69115 Heidelberg, Germany. If you have any concerns regarding our products, please contact ProductSafety@springernature.com

Printed and bound by CPI Group (UK) Ltd, Croydon, CR0 4YY
27/03/2026
02080143-0002